Distinguishing Phenomena from Their Intrinsic Nature

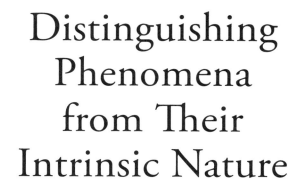

Distinguishing Phenomena from Their Intrinsic Nature

Maitreya's *Dharmadharmatāvibhaṅga*
with Commentaries by
Khenpo Shenga and Ju Mipham

TRANSLATED BY
DHARMACHAKRA TRANSLATION COMMITTEE

SNOW LION
Boston & London
2013

SNOW LION
An imprint of Shambhala Publications, Inc.
Horticultural Hall
300 Massachusetts Avenue
Boston, Massachusetts 02115
www.shambhala.com

9 8 7 6 5 4 3 2 1

First Edition
Printed in the United States of America

∞ This edition is printed on acid-free paper
that meets the American National Standards Institute z39.48 Standard.
♻ Shambhala makes every effort to print on recycled paper.
For more information please visit www.shambhala.com.

Distributed in the United States by Random House, Inc.,
and in Canada by Random House of Canada Ltd

Designed by Lora Zorian

LIBRARY OF CONGRESS CATALOGING-IN-PUBLICATION DATA
Maitreyanātha.
[Dharmadharmatāvibhaṅga. English]
Distinguishing phenomena from their intrinsic nature: Maitreya's
Dharmadharmatāvibhaṅga / with commentaries by Khenpo Shenga and Ju Mipham;
translated by Dharmachakra Translation Committee. —First Edition.
pages cm
Includes bibliographical references and index.
ISBN 978-1-55939-409-3 (hardback: alk. paper)
1. Maitreyanātha. Dharmadharmatāvibhaṅga.
I. Gźan-phan-chos-kyi-snaṅ-ba, Gźan-dga', 1871–1927.
Chos daṅ chos ñid rnam par 'byed pa'i mchan 'grel. English.
II. Mi-pham-rgya-mtsho, 'Jam-mgon 'Ju, 1846–1912.
Chos daṅ chos ñid rnam par 'byed pa'i tshigs le'ur byas pa'i 'grel pa ye śes snaṅ ba rnam
'byed. English. III. Dharmachakra Translation Committee. IV. Title.
BQ3080.D5322E535 2013
294.3'85—dc23
2012050045

CONTENTS

FOREWORD
By Chökyi Nyima Rinpoche

The protector Maitreya, lord of the Dharma and regent of the
      Victorious One,
Teaches with a flawless voice the way to distinguish
Phenomena from their intrinsic nature.
What a joy that this wish-fulfilling jewel is here today and
      remains for the future!

His excellent statements genuinely resolve
The entire treasury of profound and vast Dharma.
Their able translation and appearance in English
Is excellent fortune for sentient beings.

Offered by Chökyi Nyima, who bears the name of Tulku, on the eighth
day of the first month in the Year of the Water Dragon (March 1, 2012).

INTRODUCTION

Along with the works of Nāgārjuna and other masters of the Middle Way School, the teachings of Maitreya occupy a unique position in Tibetan Buddhism. In all four of Tibet's primary Buddhist lineages, the writings attributed to Maitreya, known popularly as Maitreya's Five Teachings,[1] are considered essential reading and are held up as masterpieces of Buddhist literature. Indeed, it is difficult to find a monastic college in Tibet where the teachings ascribed to Maitreya are not studied.

One testament to the influence of these texts is the fact that many masters from disparate schools of Buddhist thought and practice have claimed these texts as representative of their own particular views. Countless commentaries have been written on these five texts over the centuries, each presenting a unique perspective and positioning Maitreya's revelatory teachings within a broader context of Buddhist philosophy. In this volume, a companion to the previously published *Middle Beyond Extremes*, we have included one of Maitreya's most illuminating works, *Distinguishing Phenomena from Their Intrinsic Nature,*[2] along with commentaries by Khenpo Shenga[3] and Mipham Rinpoche,[4] two highly regarded masters associated with the "nonsectarian" Rimé movement in Tibet. Before we turn our attention to this text and its commentaries, let us consider the origins of Maitreya's teachings and the role of Asaṅga, Maitreya's scribe and primary commentator.

ASAṄGA AND THE TEACHINGS OF MAITREYA

The Indian saint Asaṅga was a prolific author and one of the most influential figures in Buddhist history. Along with Nāgārjuna, progenitor of the Middle Way School, he is known as one of the two "pioneers" of Buddhist philosophy, having founded a system of Buddhist thought and practice known as Yogācāra, the Yogic Practice School. In Tibet the philosophical lineages initiated by these two masters are considered the two primary forms of Great Vehicle philosophy. Their literary works continue to be at the center of the scholastic tradition of the Nyingma, Sakya, Kagyu, and Geluk schools.

According to legend, Asaṅga was born in Northwestern India (present-day Pakistan) and originally practiced as a monk in one of the lineages associated with the so-called "Lesser Vehicle." After converting to the Great Vehicle, he became inspired to spend a period of time in strict retreat and decided to focus on a form of devotional practice directed toward the future buddha Maitreya, who is believed to reside in Tuṣita Heaven awaiting the time that he will return to the world as the next fully enlightened teacher of this age. Asaṅga spent years meditating in the wilds of India. Throughout this period he was plagued by a lack of confidence and a seeming inability to progress along the path of meditation. Despite his own perception, however, Asaṅga had indeed purified his mind and was on the verge of a life-altering visionary encounter.

After twelve long years without a single vision of Maitreya, Asaṅga had lost all hope of encountering the future buddha and receiving the teachings he sought. Broken-hearted and drowning in despair, he left his retreat and wandered back to civilization, convinced that his years of practice had brought him no benefit at all. As he wandered along the road, Asaṅga came across a howling, disease-ridden dog that was covered with maggot-infested wounds. Asaṅga was overcome with compassion. His first impulse was to pick out the maggots, but he noticed that they themselves were so delicate that by picking them off the dog he would risk hurting them. Moreover, even if he were to get them off the dog unhurt, they would be deprived of their sustenance and would surely perish.

After searching for a way to help the dog without endangering the maggots, the only solution he could find was to cut off a piece of his own flesh for the maggots to feed on and to lick them off with his tongue to ensure that they would not be injured. Despite his overwhelming compassion, he found the idea of licking the maggot-infested wounds of a diseased dog revolting, so he closed his eyes and with great determination inched toward the dying dog with his tongue out. To his surprise, however, his tongue never reached the dog. When he opened his eyes he was shocked to find the future buddha Maitreya standing before him.

For years Asaṅga had yearned for such a moment, yet his first reaction to Maitreya's presence was one of indignation. "Where is your compassion?" he inquired. "I have meditated for twelve long years without so much as a single vision of you to show for it!"

"I have been with you all along," Maitreya responded, "but until this moment your mind was clouded by obscurations. The intense compassion you just experienced for the dog was enough to dissolve these obscurations, which is why you see me now. If you don't believe me, take me into the nearest village and see for yourself."

Carrying Maitreya on his shoulders, Asaṅga proceeded to a nearby settlement. Just as predicted, no one could see Maitreya, with the exception of one old woman, whose purified perception allowed her to see Maitreya in the form of the old, diseased dog that Asaṅga had encountered along the road. With this, Asaṅga finally understood that Maitreya's lack of compassion was not to blame, but rather that it was the obscurations in his own mind that had clouded his perception.

Asaṅga then pleaded with Maitreya to explain to him the sūtras of the definitive meaning. In an instant he found himself in Tuṣita Heaven, where Maitreya proceeded to share with him a set of teachings that would forever transform the landscape of Buddhist thought and practice. Asaṅga acted as Maitreya's scribe and recorded some of his teachings once he had returned from Tuṣita. When he returned to the world, he shared the teachings he had received and a new lineage was born. In time, Maitreya's Five Teachings and Asaṅga's brilliant works that unravel their profound meaning would spread throughout India, and later to China, Tibet, and beyond.[5]

DISTINGUISHING PHENOMENA FROM THEIR INTRINSIC NATURE AND THE COMMENTARIES OF KHENPO SHENGA AND JU MIPHAM

As its title indicates, the main focus of *Distinguishing Phenomena from Their Intrinsic Nature* is to clearly delineate the phenomena that comprise our ordinary, unenlightened existence (i.e., *saṃsāra*) and the intrinsic nature, or *dharmatā*, of these very same phenomena (i.e., *nirvāṇa*). In terse, cryptic verses the treatise shows how the mind enters into a state of confusion and how this process can be reversed through a fundamental transformation of the mind. At the root of our confusion, Maitreya explains, is a deeply ingrained tendency to believe that the "external" objects that populate our experience exist independent of our consciousness. This reified split between perceiving subject and perceived object sets off a chain reaction of confusion and destructive emotions, a process that perpetuates the cycle of suffering. Inquiring into the nature of this apparently dualistic experience, however, allows us to see that this is, in fact, a false distinction. At the core of Maitreya's message is the insight that this basic error of perception can be reversed by learning to see things as they are, rather than through the distorting lens of dualistic perception.

Along with Maitreya's root verses, we have included two justly famous commentaries by Khenpo Shenga and Ju Mipham. Shenga's explanation is presented as an extensive series of annotations that elaborate on the root text. As the source of these annotations, Shenga used an early commentary composed by the great Indian master Vasubandhu, who was, according to tradition, the younger brother of Asaṅga. With this format, Shenga helps the reader to understand the full import of Maitreya's teachings more readily, while at the same time not adding any commentary other than Vasubandhu's.

In contrast to Khenpo Shenga's approach, which goes straight to the source by relying on Vasubandhu's classical Indian commentary, Mipham's work offers extensive discussions on the key points of Maitreya's teachings. He begins by providing some context for the root text, showing how different commentators have categorized Maitreya's Five Teachings and presenting his own view on the place of this particular text in the overall framework of Great Vehicle philosophy. He then launches into a thorough analysis of the text, explaining everything from its title to the translator's colophon. Like many Tibetan commentaries, Mipham structures his presentation around an outline that highlights the main sections of the root text. We have included a visual representation of the outline in the Appendix. Following each section of the outline Mipham offers his own explanations, which range from pithy elucidations of Maitreya's words to lengthy discussions of difficult points in the text.

Together, these two commentaries offer a complete picture of Maitreya's profound teaching. Shenga's annotations take us back to the very origins of this sacred text in ancient India, while Mipham provides an accessible, in-depth treatment that offers a glimpse of the brilliant, syncretic mind of one of Tibet's most celebrated thinkers. In the translations that follow, each section of the root text is followed by Shenga's annotations and Mipham's commentary. Shenga's annotation-commentary appears immediately after the root verses, with the words of the root text set apart from the commentary in bold font. Mipham's commentary follows Khenpo Shenga's annotations and contains no highlighted text. See below for an example of how this text is organized.

ON THE CREATION OF THIS BOOK

In 2004, Maitreya's *Distinguishing the Middle from Extremes* was translated, along with commentaries by Khenpo Shenga and Ju Mipham, under the title *Middle Beyond Extremes: Maitreya's* Madhyāntavibhāga *with commentaries by Khenpo Shenga and Ju Mipham*. With the guidance and inspiration of Chökyi Nyima Rinpoche, this project was carried out by the Dharmachakra Translation Committee for use at the Centre for Buddhist Studies at Rangjung Yeshe Institute, a branch of Kathmandu University. This publication was the first installment in the committee's ambitious plan to translate the Thirteen Classics compiled by Khenpo Shenga.

As *Distinguishing the Middle from Extremes* was being edited for publication, Thomas Doctor also prepared a translation of the root verses of *Distinguishing Phenomena from Their Intrinsic Nature* and the commentary by Khenpo Shenga, which became the basis for a course taught by Khenpo Jampa Donden at the Centre for Buddhist Studies. At the time, our intent was to translate these two texts along with a second commentary by Ju Mipham, and to include them in a companion volume to the *Middle Beyond Extremes*. It was not until 2008 that the project resumed, at which point I returned to the texts and prepared a draft translation of Mipham's commentary, in addition to checking Thomas's translation against the original Tibetan. I then compiled and edited the texts for publication. Finally, the translations were reviewed by Zachary Beer and Thomas Doctor during a course on *Distinguishing Phenomena from Their Intrinsic Nature* taught by Tokpa Tulku at the Centre for Buddhist Studies in the spring of 2011.

The team of translators would like to express their profound gratitude to Khenpo Jampa Donden and Tokpa Tulku for providing detailed and insightful teachings on this profound text, as well as to the many other lamas who patiently answered our many questions concerning difficult points in the text. In particular, we are extremely grateful to Khenpo Sherab Sangpo and Khenpo Sherab Dorje for their expert assistance. Last but certainly not least, we would like to thank Chökyi Nyima Rinpoche, who inspired us to undertake this project and whose blessings sustained our efforts.

Our work also owes a great debt to the scholars and translators who have worked on the pioneering translations of Maitreya's teachings. In particular, we would like to acknowledge Jim Scott's excellent English translations of both the root text and Mipham's commentary,[6] and Klaus-Dieter Mathes's study and masterful German translations of the root text and commentaries by Vasubandhu and Mipham.[7] All of these works proved to be incredibly helpful as we prepared the translations included in this volume.

We would also like to acknowledge the generous support we received for this project from the Tsadra Foundation. Not only has the Tsadra Foundation made projects such as this possible, their visionary leadership in the area of Buddhist philanthropy has nurtured the traditions of practice and study that are in the process of being transmitted to the West and helped ensure that they are not lost for future generations.

The translations are based on the version of the root text contained in the Derge version of the Tibetan *Tripiṭaka*,[8] the Shenga commentary published by the Yeshe De Project,[9] and the edition of Mipham's commentary prepared under the auspices of Dilgo Khyentse.[10] For those wishing to read the commentaries back-to-back with the originals, we have made cross-referenced versions of the Tibetan texts available for download on the web site of the Dharmachakra Translation Committee, www.dharmachakra.net.

Distinguishing Phenomena from Their Intrinsic Nature is one of the great treasures of the world's spiritual heritage. Though not an easy text to study, it rewards those who take the time to penetrate its depths with a remarkable vision of reality and the potential of the human mind to divest itself of confusion and suffering. Despite our best intentions, the translations contained herein may indeed contain flaws and imperfections, and for this we offer our sincere apologies. It is our hope that this book may provide a gateway for those wishing to access these seminal teachings and the great wisdom traditions that they have inspired. May whatever virtue that results from producing this book cause goodness to reign in all times and places, and may it serve to ensure the long lives and flourishing activity of the precious masters who embody these teachings.

On behalf of the translation team,
CORTLAND DAHL
Minneapolis, United States, 2011

ধর্মধর্মতাবিভঙ্গকারিকা বিবরণনিয়

ཆོས་དང་ཆོས་ཉིད་རྣམ་པར་འབྱེད་པའི་ཚིག་ལེའུར་བྱེད་པའི་མཆན་འགྲེལ་བཞུགས་སོ།

ত্রীমক্রন্নতামাবিভঙ্গ ধর্মধর্মতাবিভঙ্গকারিকা বিবরণনিয়

ཆོས་དང་ཆོས་ཉིད་རྣམ་པར་འབྱེད་པའི་ཚིག་ལེའུར་བྱེད་པའི་འགྲེལ་པ་ཡེ་ཤེས་སྣང་བ་ཞེས་བྱ་བ་བཞུགས་སོ།

MAITREYA'S DISTINGUISHING PHENOMENA FROM THEIR INTRINSIC NATURE

ELUCIDATED BY

Shenphen Nangwa

Annotation-commentary on the Stanzas on
Distinguishing Phenomena from Their Intrinsic Nature

AND

Ju Mipham

Distinguishing Wakefulness from Appearance—
A Commentary on the Treatise
Distinguishing Phenomena from Their Intrinsic Nature

The vajra of your nonconceptual wakefulness completely destroyed
The mountain of apprehended and apprehender,
Bringing the attainment of the inconceivable body of wakefulness—
Supreme Teacher Śākyamuni, to you I bow down.

Heir to the victorious ones, Mañjuśrī,
Holder of the treasury of profound and vast Dharma,
Along with regent Maitreya, master of the tenth ground—
The nails of your toes I take as my crown jewels.

Here I shall explain the great treatise
That elucidates the profound reality
Of nonconceptual wakefulness, the essence
Of all the treasuries of the Great Vehicle's teachings.

The noble bodhisattva Asaṅga performed the practice of Lord Maitreya for twelve human years before meeting Maitreya face-to-face. Leading him to the heavenly realm of Tuṣita, Maitreya presented Asaṅga with five teachings that expound upon the intent of all the words of the Victorious One. These five teachings are the Two Ornaments, the Two Treatises That Distinguish, and *The Supreme Continuity*.

Some individuals hold these five to be a single treatise. Others refute the notion that these five works form the body of one scripture by showing that their teachings are incompatible with one another in the final analysis, demonstrating, for example, that they include varying positions concerning whether there is only one vehicle or three vehicles in terms of the definitive meaning.

For this reason they hold that each treatise has its own approach and is a commentary on a distinct teaching of the Buddha. Some, for instance, hold that the first and last treatises listed above explain Middle Way thought, while the remaining three pertain to the Mind Only School. Others hold that only the *Ornament of the Sūtras* is a Mind Only scripture and that the remaining four are all associated with the Middle Way. Yet another position holds that only the *Ornament of Manifest Realization* is a Middle Way treatise, while the other four are works of the Mind Only School. There are also those who believe that all five are in line with Mind Only thought, some who believe just the opposite, and so on.

In actuality, however, it is indisputable that the *Ornament of Manifest Realization* comments on the thought of the Transcendent Insight, the middle teaching of the Buddha, and that *The Supreme Continuity* comments on the thought of the definitive meaning of the final wheel of Dharma, the sūtras on buddha nature. Both of these treatises hold that there is but one family and one vehicle in the final analysis, a view that is in line with the thought of the Middle Way. The *Ornament of the Sūtras*, on the other hand, explains the thought of most of those sūtras not addressed by the aforementioned two scriptures, doing so in a single presentation. It is clear that, for the most part, this treatise highlights the thought of Mind Only sūtras, in that it does not treat the accounts of the single class and the single vehicle as definitive, for example.

The Two Treatises That Distinguish teach on the vast and profound aspects of the Great Vehicle in general. Though they do indeed offer extensive presentations of the principle of the three natures and how external objects do not exist, this alone does not warrant their categorization as exclusively Mind Only scriptures. Indeed, there is no conflict in using the Dharma terminology employed in these works to present the thought of the Middle Way as well. On this point, *The Sūtra of the Journey to Laṅkā* states:

> The five principles and three natures,
> Along with the eight collections of consciousness
> And the twofold absence of self —
> The entirety of the Great Vehicle is subsumed in these.

Hence, such terminology is used to encompass the entirety of the Great Vehicle. This is also evidenced by the fact that the terminology associated with the three essential natures is found in *The Sūtra*

Requested by Maitreya, a scripture that elucidates the thought of the Mother [of Transcendent Insight].

Moreover, we do not find any statements or reasonings that would necessitate accepting the position that nondual consciousness is truly established, as the Mind Only scriptural tradition holds. For this reason, not only is there no problem whatsoever in explaining these texts to be impartial commentaries on the thought of the Great Vehicle in general, this is actually reflected in their structure. Hence, *Distinguishing the Middle from Extremes* is a scripture that elucidates the principles of the vast path of the three vehicles, while *Distinguishing Phenomena from Their Intrinsic Nature* is a scripture that enables one to ascertain nonconceptual wakefulness, the essential subject matter of all the profound collections of sūtras, in harmony with the union of the two truths as taught in the Middle Way School of Yogic Practice.

For this reason, and also due to their extreme profundity, both this scripture and *The Supreme Continuity* were bound with a seal of secrecy and eventually were no longer extant in India. Later, the master Maitrīpa observed light emerging from the crack in a stupa, whereupon he extracted the manuscripts of *Distinguishing Phenomena from Their Intrinsic Nature* and *The Supreme Continuity*. These two works then flourished once again.

When Shama Lotsawa Sengé Gyaltsen requested to translate this scripture, his paṇḍita stressed its importance, giving him one page at a time with the words, "Do not let this work go to waste. Due to its strict seal this is a rare scripture. If it were to disappear, it would be as though the lord Maitreya had passed away from Jambudvīpa!" As alluded to here, the profound reality taught by this text is the definitive secret of the view.

Since it is necessary for all practitioners of the Great Vehicle to realize this view, there is nothing inappropriate in explaining this scripture from the perspective of either the Middle Way or Mind Only School. Despite the fact that masters of both the Middle Way and Mind Only traditions have explained them to be texts that explicate their own respective positions, the intent of the Sūtras on Transcendent Insight is that of the Middle Way. In the same way, there are those who believe that this treatise teaches the view of Mind Only, and insofar as such individuals are

operating according to their own intellectual capacity, there is no contradiction in that. In actuality, however, this scripture offers a precise and ex-
plicit presentation of nonconceptual wakefulness, the ultimate, profound
meaning of the Great Vehicle. In this sense, it is a general commentary on
the entire range of profound sūtras.

While its position on relative subjects is in harmony with Mind
Only, this work's assertions concerning the ultimate—the inherent nature—are in line with the Middle Way. Thus, in the final analysis, its
intent is that of the Middle Way, yet it uses the principle of the union of
the Middle Way and Mind Only to teach the vital points of the view of
the Great Vehicle. When understood and explained in this manner, the
full import of this great treatise will have been thoroughly elucidated.

This great treatise can be explained in four sections:

1. The meaning of the title
2. The translator's homage
3. The meaning of the scripture
4. The meaning of the conclusion

THE TITLE

In the Indian language: Dharmadharmatā vibhaṅga kārikā

**In the Tibetan language: Chos dang chos nyid rnam par
'byed pa tshig le'ur byas pa**

The first section concerns the meaning of the title. When translated
into Tibetan, the Sanskrit term *dharma* becomes "phenomena" [*chos*],
dharmatā becomes "intrinsic nature" [*chos nyid*], *vibhaṅga* becomes
"distinguishing" [*rnam par 'byed pa*], and *kārikā* becomes "presented in
stanzas" [*tshig le'ur byas pa*]. Hence, the title indicates that this treatise
accurately depicts the character of phenomena and their intrinsic nature.
In other words, it delineates cyclic existence and the transcendence of
suffering, distinguishing them from one another in a precise manner.

THE TRANSLATOR'S HOMAGE

Homage to the protector Maitreya.

The translators began their project to translate this text by showing respect via the three gates, stating, "We pay *homage to* the author of this very text, *the* great bodhisattva and *protector* of all beings, *Maitreya*, who currently resides in Tuṣita and is referred to as such because he possesses great love."[1] Maitreya has been known by this name from the time he became a bodhisattva and will continue to be until he attains buddhahood, from which he is separated by only a single birth.

THE MEANING OF THE SCRIPTURE

The meaning of this scripture is discussed in two sections: (1) the stanza that relates to the composition of the treatise and (2) the actual body of the treatise.

THE COMPOSITION OF THE TREATISE

On the first topic, the treatise states:

> **Something is to be understood and entirely relinquished,**
> **While something else is to be directly perceived.**
> **Hence this treatise has been composed**
> **With the wish to distinguish the characteristics of these.**

Something, meaning the phenomena that are the factors of thorough affliction, **is to be understood and entirely relinquished, while something else,** meaning the intrinsic nature that is distinguished with reference to a fundamental transformation characterized by complete purification, **is to be directly perceived. Hence this treatise has been composed with the wish to distinguish the characteristics of these** two. Thus, it is implied that this is not a distinction made between different objects.

The something that is to be understood and entirely relinquished is cyclic existence, while the something else that is to be actualized is the transcendence of suffering. Because all entities that are known and either relinquished or pursued by beings fall into one of these two categories, the noble Maitreya states, "This great treatise has been composed with vast insight and compassion, with the wish to distinguish precisely and unerringly the characteristics of cyclic existence from those of the transcendence of suffering."

The Actual Body of the Treatise

Second, the body of the treatise is discussed in three sections: (1) a brief presentation, (2) a detailed explanation, and (3) a concluding summary that uses metaphors to illustrate the principles outlined in the text.

A Brief Presentation

The first section is further divided into (1) an identification of the essence of cyclic existence and the transcendence of suffering, (2) individual explanations of their respective characteristics, (3) the underlying rationale for these characteristics, and (4) an investigation into whether these two are the same or different.

THE ESSENCE OF CYCLIC EXISTENCE AND THE TRANSCENDENCE OF SUFFERING

On the first topic, the treatise states:

> If all of these are summarized,
> They can be understood to be twofold
> Because everything is included in
> Phenomena and their intrinsic nature.
>
> That which is classified as phenomena
> Is cyclic existence, whereas the intrinsic nature

Is classified as the transcendence of suffering
Of the three vehicles.

One may wonder whether or not this is nothing more than a discussion of the distinctions between phenomena and their intrinsic nature, or whether these two are all that there is. This is not a twofold distinction that is made in isolation from the multiplicity of things, for the Transcendent Conqueror has employed classifications in terms of aggregates and so forth. **If all of these are summarized, they can be understood to be twofold because everything is included in** the **phenomena** that are characterized by thorough affliction **and their intrinsic nature**, which is characterized by fundamental transformation.

It may be said, "Through this we will not know the distinction between that which constitutes cyclic existence and that which constitutes the transcendence of suffering."

In response, it is said, "**That which is classified as phenomena is cyclic existence, whereas the intrinsic nature is classified as the transcendence of suffering of the three vehicles.**"

When all of the topics contained in the Buddha's sublime words are summarized, they can be understood to be twofold. Everything, meaning all that can be known, is subsumed by phenomena and their intrinsic nature. If these two are thoroughly understood, one will no longer remain ignorant regarding any of the topics contained in the Buddha's sublime words.

In this context, that which is classified as phenomena is cyclic existence, in the sense of the dualistic perception of apprehended and apprehender. The reason is that this encompasses all the phenomena that appear to delusion. It is the nature of these phenomena that is to be known by those who seek liberation and omniscience. They function as the basis for the process of relinquishment carried out by those same individuals.

That which is classified as the intrinsic nature, on the other hand, is the transcendence of suffering of the three vehicles. All that is to be genuinely understood and actualized comes down to this. By virtue of seeing that there are no essences in terms of personal selves or phenomena within cyclic existence, regardless of how things may appear, a transcendence of suffering is achieved that involves a fundamental transformation. Since here one has genuinely accessed the way things are, there is no discrepancy between the way things appear and the way they are.

THE CHARACTERISTICS OF CYCLIC EXISTENCE AND THE TRANSCENDENCE OF SUFFERING

This second section includes discussions of (1) the characteristics of phenomena and (2) the characteristics of their intrinsic nature.

THE CHARACTERISTICS OF PHENOMENA

On the first, the treatise states:

> Here phenomena are defined as the appearances
> Of duality and of things expressed—
> The appearances of the false imagination.
> They appear yet do not exist.
> Therefore, they are false.
> These as well are entirely nonexistent in actuality.
> Since they are merely concepts, they are imaginary.

It may be said, "That may be so, but because their characteristics have not been expressed, the characteristics of phenomena cannot be known."

Here phenomena are defined as the appearances of the duality of the entities of apprehended and apprehender and of things expressed through the imputations of essences and distinctions, i.e., the appearances of the false imagination. They merely appear, yet while doing so do not exist. Therefore, they are false. These as well are entirely nonexistent in actuality. Since they are merely concepts and only exist as deluded appearances, they are imaginary.

In the preceding discussion, cyclic existence was referred to as "phenomena." Here phenomena are defined as the dualistic appearance of apprehended and apprehender and of "things expressed." The latter refers to the expressions that are made by means of various names in seeming accordance with the way things appear. Just like the appearance of depth in a well-crafted painting, the dualistic appearances of apprehended and apprehender do occur, yet they do not have any actual establishment. These are falsely imagined because they appear to the mind yet do not exist in actuality, as is the case with falling hairs and other such examples. Therefore, they, meaning these appearances of duality, do exist in the sense that they appear, yet they are false in actuality.

For this reason, though the subjective mind refers to things as this and that and makes imputations based on those appearances of duality, these expressions and imputations are also entirely devoid of establishment in terms of the actuality that they are meant to express. Indeed, since they are merely one's own conceptual imputations, whatever we may refer to as phenomena is mere imagination. To summarize, what is being taught here is that all the phenomena that appear in a dualistic manner and are fixated on as such are nothing more than imputations. They may appear, yet they have no nature of their own.

THE CHARACTERISTICS OF THEIR INTRINSIC NATURE

On the second topic, the treatise states:

> Furthermore, the intrinsic nature is defined
> As suchness, in which there is no distinction
> Between apprehended and apprehender,
> The expressed and that which expresses.

> Furthermore, the intrinsic nature is defined as suchness, in which there is no distinction between apprehended and apprehender, and no distinction in terms of the expressed and that which expresses.

The intrinsic nature is the opposite of what was just taught. It is defined as suchness, the object of individual self-awareness. In suchness there are no distinctions in terms of an apparent duality of apprehended and apprehender, and in the absence of dualistic appearances neither is there any distinction to be made in terms of an expressed meaning and words that express it.

THE UNDERLYING RATIONALE FOR THESE CHARACTERISTICS

On the third topic, the treatise states:

> Since the nonexistent appears,
> Delusion is the cause of thorough affliction
> Because, while an illusory elephant and so forth may appear,
> That which exists does not.
> If either nonexistence or appearance were nonexistent,
> Delusion and the absence of delusion,
> As well as thorough affliction and complete purification,
> Would not make sense.

Since the nonexistent characteristics of phenomena presented above do indeed appear, delusion is the cause of thorough affliction because the three types of thorough affliction occur due to the overt fixation on these factors. While an illusory elephant, jewels, grains, and so forth may appear, that twofold absence of self, which in fact exists, does not.

It may be asked, "Of nonexistence and appearance, why is one not held to be nonexistent?"

If either nonexistence or appearance were nonexistent, delusion and the absence of delusion, as well as thorough affliction and complete purification, would not make sense. In other words, if there were only nonexistence and no appearance, there could be no delusion because [appearance itself] would be absent and one would not be deluded concerning nonexistence. If there were no delusion, there could be no freedom from delusion either, for freedom from delusion is preceded by delusion. In the same way, there could not be any thorough affliction because it is caused by delusion. Finally, without thorough affliction there could not be any complete purification either, for complete purification is preceded by thorough affliction. Thus, everyone would be effortlessly liberated, which contradicts what we know to be the case through perception.

On the other hand, if there were only appearance and no non-existence, there could not be any delusion either. Since nonexistence would not exist, that which appears to be the case would be thoroughly established and, hence, not delusion. The remaining consequences would apply in the same way.

Next we shall establish the rationale for these appearances that do not exist in reality. Since entities appear while being nonexistent in actuality, as is the case with hallucinations brought about by a disease, these deluded appearances are the cause of all thorough affliction. The reason here is that dualistic fixation manifests based on dualistic appearance. This fixation, in turn, gives rise to various habitual tendencies. Just like the form of an illusory elephant conjured up by magical spells and substances, or a beautiful woman in a dream, these phenomena appear yet do not exist. That which does exist from the outset, namely the way in which things are devoid of the two forms of self, does not appear to ordinary beings, who are under the influence of such unreal appearances.

Because this is the case, cyclic existence and the transcendence of suffering, as well as delusion and liberation, are tenable. If this were not the case, these principles would not make sense. If the lack of existence in actuality, paired with the appearance of that which does not exist, did not occur together, and instead one of these were not present, delusion and nondelusion would be completely untenable, as would thorough affliction and complete purification.

If things were not nonexistent in actuality, but instead existed and were established in the dualistic manner in which they appear, it would not be reasonable for fixating on them in this way to be deluded or mistaken. Moreover, since there would be no such thing as a method for averting delusion, the transcendence of suffering would be nonexistent in every respect.

If [the occurrence of] appearances were as nonexistent as they are in actuality, it would not be possible for anyone to be subject to the delusion of apprehended and apprehender. In the absence of delusion, moreover, its opposite—complete purification—would also be nonexistent, just as one cannot cut the nonexistent horn of a rabbit.

Therefore, since nonexistence and appearance occur together, the thorough affliction of mistakenly believing in the existence of the nonexistent is possible. Likewise, it is also possible to attain the transcendence of suffering by virtue of the path on which one is freed from delusion by knowing the nonexistent to be nonexistent.

ARE PHENOMENA AND THEIR INTRINSIC NATURE THE SAME OR DIFFERENT?

On the fourth topic, the treatise states:

> These two are neither
> The same nor different
> Because the existent and nonexistent
> Have differences as well as none.

It may then be asked, "Are phenomena and their intrinsic nature one and the same or different?"

These two, phenomena and their intrinsic nature, are neither the same nor different because the existent, the intrinsic nature, and the nonexistent, phenomena, have differences, (and thus cannot be the same) as well as none, for the intrinsic nature is distinguished as the mere nonexistence of phenomena (and thus these two cannot be different either).

Cyclic existence and the transcendence of suffering, or phenomena and their intrinsic nature, are neither identical in essence, nor essentially different. How so? The intrinsic nature, the transcendence of suffering that is completely pure by its very nature, exists from the outset as the way things are. The phenomena that possess this nature, on the other hand, meaning the phenomena of cyclic existence, appear in a dualistic manner but are not what they seem in terms of the way things are. In this sense there is a difference between these two. Thus, conventionally speaking, phenomena and their intrinsic nature are not the same.

It must also be understood that these two are not different either. If one did not exist, neither would the remaining factor. Similarly, aside from the intrinsic nature being delineated by the mere lack of establishment of phenomena in reality, these two are not distinct from one another. Indeed, the distinction between the existent intrinsic nature and the nonexistent phenomena that possess it is relative. Other than being what must be accepted and rejected, respectively, there is not even the slightest existence of any essence that would establish these two as different objects.

Detailed Explanation

The second section contains two divisions: (1) a detailed explanation of phenomena and (2) a detailed explanation of their intrinsic nature.

Phenomena

The first topic is divided further into (1) a presentation of the topics and (2) an explanation of each individual topic.

A Presentation of the Topics

On the first, the treatise states:

> The sixfold access
> To phenomena is supreme
> Because it allows for the full access
> To characteristics, establishment,
> The absence of sameness and difference,
> The shared basis and the unshared,
> And the nonexistence of what appears
> To be apprehended and apprehender.

Of these two—phenomena and their intrinsic nature—which are not different from one another, how should one access phenomena, or how may one access phenomena well?

The sixfold access to phenomena explained here **is supreme because it allows for the full access to (1) characteristics, (2) establishment, (3) the absence of sameness and difference, (4) the shared basis and (5) the unshared, and (6) the nonexistence of what appears to be apprehended and apprehender.**

The sixfold approach to understanding outlined here involves relating to phenomena via study and contemplation. This is the supreme way to ascertain these phenomena. The reasoning here is that this approach allows one to access the nature of the samsaric phenomena that are meant to be relinquished, whereby one may ascertain the entire range [of such phenomena] with ease.

These six ways of relating to phenomena are as follows: (1) relating to the objects of one's understanding, i.e., the characteristics of samsaric phenomena; (2) demonstrating how the characteristics of these phenomena are established as such; (3) understanding and relating to the way in which phenomena and their intrinsic nature are neither the same nor different; (4) understanding the shared abode of cyclic existence; (5) understanding how this abode is not shared; and (6) understanding how to thoroughly access the fact of the nonexistence of what appears to be apprehended and apprehender. Presenting phenomena in terms of these six allows one to fully understand the issue.

THE MEANING OF EACH INDIVIDUAL TOPIC

The second section (1) shows how the first three topics have already been taught and (2) explains the last three topics.

THE FIRST THREE TOPICS

Concerning the first, the treatise states:

Of these, characteristics, establishment,
And the absence of sameness and difference
Are as was briefly taught.

Of these six, (1) **characteristics,** (2) the **establishment** of the
result, **and** (3) **the absence of sameness and difference are** to
be understood **as was briefly taught** in the verses that read: (1)
". . . The appearances of the false imagination," (2) "If either
nonexistence or appearance were nonexistent . . . ," and (3)
"These two are neither / The same nor different . . ."

Of the six factors to access presented here, characteristics, establishment, and the absence of sameness and difference are to be understood
as was explained briefly above.

THE LAST THREE TOPICS

This second section is divided into explanations of (1) the two abodes
and (2) how to relate to the reality of the absence of apprehended and
apprehender.

THE TWO ABODES

The first explanation is divided further into (1) a summary of both in
common and (2) extensive individual explanations of the significance
of each.

A SUMMARY OF SHARED AND UNSHARED ABODES

Concerning the first, the treatise states:

That which cycles and where the cycling takes place
Abide throughout as the constituents
Of sentient beings and their environment.
The constituents of the environment appear shared

And are, as such, shared awareness.
The constituents of sentient beings
Are shared, but also unshared.

The phenomena of cyclic existence are **that which cycles and where the cycling takes place.** These **abide** pervasively **throughout as the constituents of sentient beings and their environment. The constituents of the environment appear** as a **shared** experience **and are, as such,** the **shared** appearances of **awareness.** They are shared awareness because the consciousness associated with such appearances arises within the individual mind streams of all sentient beings. **The constituents of sentient beings are shared, but also unshared.**

The constituents of sentient beings are that which cycles, while the constituents of the environment are the context within which this continuous cycling takes place in the form of rebirth. The world of sentient beings and the world of the environment are known as the abodes throughout which beings cycle. Aside from these two—the supported constituents of sentient beings and the constituents of the environment that is their support—there is no other abode of cyclic existence whatsoever.

"Of these," one may wonder, "what is shared and what is not?"

The constituents of the world's environment are referred to as "shared abodes" insofar as they appear collectively to those sentient beings whose active habitual tendencies correspond with one another and who have corresponding perceptions, or consciousnesses. The phenomena that comprise the constituents of sentient beings, however, are both shared and not shared.

The second section contains explanations of (1) shared abodes and (2) those that are not shared.

SHARED ABODES

Concerning the first of these, the treatise states:

Furthermore, birth, conventions,
Support, subjugation, benefit, harm,
Good qualities, and flaws
Mutually cause one another by ruling.
They are, therefore, shared.

Furthermore, **birth,** looking and other **conventions,** the **support** or **subjugation** enacted by others, **benefit**ing and **harm**ing others, learning and other **good qualities, and flaws** like desire are present in individual mind streams. These factors **mutually cause one another by** being the **ruling** conditions for one another. **They are, therefore,** classified as constituents of sentient beings that are **shared.**

The phenomena categorized as the constituents of sentient beings can be classified as follows: (1) womb birth, (2) perceptible physical and verbal conventions, (3) supporting or (4) subjugating another, (5) benefiting, (6) harming, (7) the arising of the positive qualities associated with learning and other such factors that depend upon another and (8) the occurrence of flaws like desire. For a consciousness that manifests in this manner to occur, sentient beings must serve as the ruling conditions for one another and, thereby, mutually cause one another. For this reason they are termed "shared appearances." Birth, for example, occurs as a shared experience insofar as one's karma functions as the cause and the seeds of one's parents as the simultaneous conditions. This shared cause, in turn, results in a body born from the womb coming into existence.

Likewise, shared conventions involve observing and communicating with others, as well as other such activities that are instigated by another individual's physical or verbal communication. This is the case when one person cares for another in either a spiritual or material sense; defeats them in an argument, in combat, or otherwise; helps them by protecting them from something they are afraid of or benefiting them in another way; harms them by beating them or through some other form of violence; develops positive qualities through study; or creates faults by teaching negative views, arousing desire, and so on. Thus, situations where one individual acts as the ruling condition and the phenomena of another person's mind stream function as the primary cause are referred to as "shared" from the perspective of there being a single shared result.

Conventionally these results are brought about by a collection of causes and conditions. In actuality, however, using the term "ruling cause" also indicates that there are no collectively experienced external objects. The reason, here, is that there are no external objects to function as observed conditions aside from consciousness, nor are the external environment or other seemingly shared appearances anything more than the objective aspect of the inner consciousness.

Unshared Abodes

On the second topic, the treatise states:

> Abode, awareness, pleasure, pain,
> Karma, death, transference,
> Birth, bondage, and liberation
> Are not shared.
> Hence, these are unshared abodes.

"Well, what then is not shared?" one may ask.

The **abode**, meaning the all-ground consciousness; the **aware-ness**, i.e., the engaged consciousnesses; **pleasure** and **pain**; virtu-ous, nonvirtuous, and neutral **karma**; **death** and **transference**; **birth**; and **bondage and liberation are not shared.** In this way, because they are not embodied, and because they are to be cog-nized individually, these factors are not causes for the arising of corresponding awarenesses within distinct mind streams. **Hence, these are unshared abodes** and so on.

The abode—meaning the all-ground consciousness; the seven collec-tions of awareness; the individual experiences of pleasure and pain; the karma accumulated through intention; death and transference; taking birth in an individual existence; and being both bound in and liberated from cyclic existence are all unshared phenomena within individual mind streams. These unshared experiential factors within individual mind streams are not experienced in common with other sentient beings. Hence, these are the unshared abodes of sentient beings.

THE NONEXISTENCE OF APPREHENDED AND APPREHENDER

This second section contains two discussions: (1) an explanation of the tenet of mere awareness in the absence of external referents and (2) how to access the reality of there being neither apprehended nor apprehender independent of awareness.

AN EXPLANATION OF THE TENET OF MERE AWARENESS IN THE ABSENCE OF EXTERNAL REFERENTS

The first topic contains two further divisions: (1) showing that there is no apprehended object independent of what apprehends it and (2) how to dispense with any uncertainties.

THERE IS NO APPREHENDED OBJECT APART FROM WHAT APPREHENDS IT

Concerning the first topic, the treatise states:

> The appearance of a shared, externally apprehended object
> Is the apprehending awareness.
> Apart from consciousness
> There is no external object
> Because it is shared.

In terms of accessing the nonexistence of the apparent apprehended and apprehender, **the appearance of a shared, externally apprehended object is the apprehending awareness** of a distinct stream of being. When it appears to an apprehending awareness, **apart from consciousness there is no external object.** Why? **Because it is the shared** awareness of the environment. Thus, although an awareness that takes the form of this experience arises in individual mind streams, the awareness of one is not the object of another.

Those with overt fixation on external objects may entertain the following thought: "No one can deny the presence of material objects, such as mountains and all the other things that we collectively observe. For this very reason, outer objects do indeed exist."

This, however, is not the case. Let us take as our subject a mountain or another object that appears collectively as an externally apprehended object. Such an object is not established by virtue of its own essence as an external, material object that is something other than the inner consciousness that perceives it. Why? Because it is the very inner apprehending awareness of those whose active habitual tendencies correspond with one another that appears as various outer objects, just like the imagery in dreams.

Therefore, there are no external objects apart from consciousness. What we refer to as "collectively observed external objects" are appearances that manifest collectively to various individuals with distinct streams of being and, hence, nothing more than the perceptions of individual streams of being.

"What is the reason for this?" one may ask.

The so-called "collectively observed objects" that supposedly prove the existence of outer objects are posited to be "collectively experienced outer objects" merely because they appear in a similar manner to the conditioned perspective of individual mind streams. There is nothing more to it than that. These appearances are the perceptions of the individual mind streams that witness them. It is utterly impossible for them to be shared. A so-called "outer object" that is something other than such a mere appearance and that is collectively experienced can never be logically established as such. Otherwise, one would have to posit the existence of the object apart from its appearance to a mind. It does not, however, make sense to posit something that cannot appear, since there would be no valid cognition by which such an object could be evaluated.

If we carefully analyze these so-called "collectively observed phenomena," we will find that the reason for positing them as such is that they appear in a similar manner to distinct mind streams. Nevertheless, while these appearances may be similar, this does not necessitate there being a single, collectively experienced outer object that causes their appearance, just as people whose vision has been distorted by a magician's spells may have similar experiences. For those beings whose active habitual tendencies correspond with one another, the abode and other such factors may appear in a similar manner so long as the potency of these habitual tendencies has not run out. However, no cause of these corresponding appearances truly exists outside [of the minds that perceive them]. Just as each of the six classes of beings perceives the same water differently, in accord with its karmic perceptions, it should be understood that such appearances are nothing more than the self-appearances of one's own inner mind.

Dispensing with Uncertainties

On the second topic, the treatise states:

> Its counterpart is the apprehended
> Object of awareness that is not shared—
> The minds and so forth of others.
> These are not the mutual objects
> Of apprehending awarenesses,
> Whether out of meditative equipoise or within,
> Because, for those not in equipoise,
> It is their thoughts that appear,
> Whereas for those who are in equipoise,
> It is a reflection of these that appears
> Within the field of a particular absorption.

Its counterpart is the apprehended object of awareness that is not shared—the minds and so forth of others (thus including mental states). These are not the mutual objects of apprehending awarenesses, whether these awarenesses are out of meditative equipoise or within equipoise. This is because,

for those who are **not in equipoise, it is their thoughts that appear** (and thus the object is not the mind and so forth of others), **whereas for those who are in equipoise, it is a reflection of these that appears within the field of a particular absorption** (and thus the object is not the minds and so forth of others). Therefore, because it is one's own awareness that is the object, no objects exist external to consciousness, and because no such objects exist, that which appears to be apprehended is nonexistent as well.

"All that appears is indeed merely what appears in the mind," one may object. "No one can refute this. Nevertheless, this does not prove that all appearances are substantially identical to the mind, nor does it prove that there are no outer objects associated with the appearances one observes. For instance, one person's mind can be directly perceived by another, yet this does not prove that the other person's mind stream does not exist or that the appearance of this mind is substantially identical to one's own mind. The same can then be said concerning outer objects."

In response we may argue as follows. In addition to cognitions of the world of the environment and other seemingly shared experiences, there are also apprehended objects of awareness, or consciousness, that are not shared: the minds, mental events, and so forth that comprise the mind streams of other sentient beings. Such a consciousness may indeed accurately cognize the minds of other individuals through the power of knowledge mantras, meditative absorption, and so forth. However, regardless of whether or not the subject is resting in meditative equipoise, it is not the case that the apprehending awareness is actually taking another mind stream as its object. How so? For those not in equipoise, it is their own thought activity that appears in a manner that resembles another individual's mind, while for those in equipoise, it is a reflection of the other individual's mind that appears within the experiential domain of their meditative absorption, similar in form to knowing the past or future. In other words, it is merely an image that resembles the other person's mind.

Therefore, the way the mind may take on the features of an object that it observes is different from cognizing an object in such a way that the mind itself is substantially identical to the object. Therefore, there are two different modes of cognition: one in which the mind takes on the features of the object it observes and another in which the mind arises in a way that is substantially identical to that object. For instance, a yogi may observe the happiness, suffering, or some other state of an ordinary mind and be cognizant of it as such, while not having a comparable experience him- or herself.

"Well, while it may indeed be the case that outer objects are not directly experienced," one may counter, "they can still be experienced through the arising of certain features, as was the case with another individual's mind. How would that present any problem?"

In response, we may say that consciousness itself manifests in a manner that resembles an object due to the activation of internal habitual tendencies. Moreover, without such habitual tendencies outer objects would not appear, even if we were to grant that they exist. This we can see to be the case with hungry ghosts and water and those in the realm of boundless space and forms. When internal habitual tendencies become active, on the other hand, a discrete outer object need not be present, as we can see to be the case with hungry ghosts who perceive pus and the all-pervasive space perceived by those in the realm of infinite space. Therefore, it is clear that appearances occur due to the mind; mind does not occur due to appearances. Similarly, it is not that the mind stream of one person occurs due to the mind of someone else, since one cannot accept the position that one person transcending suffering would necessitate everyone transcending suffering.

"Well then," one may respond, "since all phenomena are directly perceptible to the buddhas, if what appeared to them were substantially identical to their wakefulness, then buddhas and sentient beings would turn out to be of one single mind stream."

In the case of the Buddha, the notion of a mind stream that is different from that of sentient beings is not relevant. Since this is the wakefulness of complete transformation that accords with the intrinsic nature of things, it is impossible to make delineations concerning sameness, difference, or otherwise. On this point, it is taught:

Unborn and unceasing,
The intrinsic nature is the same as nirvana.

How to Access the Absence of Apprehended and Apprehender

On the second topic, the treatise states:

> Once it has been established that what appears to be
>   apprehended does not exist,
> It has also been established that what appears to apprehend
>   does not exist either.
> Due to this, access to the nonexistence
> Of what appears as apprehended and apprehender
> Is established because of the full emergence
> Of that which has no beginning.
> The reason for this is that the complete lack of establishment
> Of duality is fully established.

Once it has been established that what appears to be apprehended does not exist, it has also been established that what appears to apprehend does not exist either. In other words, "without anything apprehended there cannot be any apprehender." Due to this reason, access to the nonexistence of what appears as apprehended and apprehender is established because of the full emergence of the grasping of apprehended and apprehender that is due to that which has no beginning, the habitual tendencies. The reason for this is that, despite the complete lack of establishment of the duality of apprehended and apprehender, one witnesses the arising of a consciousness that is in conflict [with that lack of establishment] and so on. For this reason it is fully established.

If what appears to be apprehended does not exist by its very own essence apart from that which apprehends it, then what appears to be the apprehender does not exist either. The reason, here, is that the apprehender exists in relation to the apprehended, not in isolation. Therefore, awareness is devoid of both apprehender and apprehended, in all their various forms. Free from subject and object, by its very own nature awareness is a mere indescribable luminosity. It is no different from the thoroughly established suchness that is empty of the two forms of self. Since even proponents of the Mind Only School must realize this, why mention that it must also be realized by followers of the Middle Way?

According to the Mind Only School, the significance of all sixteen forms of emptiness is perfectly complete within this nature. Since it cannot be conceived of or expressed as being outer, inner, or any other dualistic phenomena, it is held to be beyond elaborations.

Nevertheless, a subtle vestige of a realist philosophical tenet does remain concerning this ineffable consciousness. This position holds that the essence of this consciousness truly exists. Yet if this view is undermined using reasoning and one instead asserts that the mind devoid of apprehended and apprehender is itself not truly existent—that this mind is in a state of union with emptiness, primordially pure and luminous—one has arrived at the genuine Middle Way. Therefore, we may draw a distinction between these two Great Vehicle schools, the Middle Way and Mind Only, in terms of whether or not this subtle level of fixation has been eliminated or not. Aside from this, however, in terms of the practice of formal meditation and postmeditation there is a great deal of similarity between these two schools, so much so that even the great scholars and saints of the Noble Land of India did not differentiate between these two when it came to the practice of the Great Vehicle.

As explained above, by understanding how the duality of the apprehended and apprehender does not exist, one may rest one-pointedly in the nature of this nonexistence, whereby one may directly access the nonexistence of what appears to be the apprehended and apprehender. In other words, one will behold the nondual intrinsic nature.

"It does not," one may object, "make sense that this sort of nondual intrinsic nature is thoroughly established from the beginning. Given its existence, it could not fail to manifest, and there could therefore not be any delusion of dualistic appearances."

This, however, is not the case. The habitual tendencies associated with the dualistic appearances of apprehender and apprehended have been in operation throughout beginningless time. Serving to obscure thatness, these tendencies have been present alongside the mind's luminous nature. As these habitual tendencies fully emerge, meaning that they become active or ripen, they cause delusion and cyclic existence to occur.

"Well then," one may continue, "if they have existed alongside this nature throughout time without beginning, then wouldn't it be impossible to eliminate them?"

This as well is not the case because the apprehended and apprehender's lack of full establishment is itself completely established. Once one has realized this and meditated upon it, it will be seen in actuality.

This has presented the underlying rationale for accessing nonduality.

AN EXTENSIVE EXPLANATION OF THE INTRINSIC NATURE

This second section contains two further divisions: (1) a summary using headings and (2) a detailed explanation of the meaning of these headings. Concerning the first, the treatise states:

> These six ways of accessing
> The intrinsic nature are unsurpassed
> Because they access the characteristics,
> The basis, ascertainment, contact,
> Recollection, and having become
> Of the identity of that.

Accessing the intrinsic nature is explained next. On this topic, [it is said], **These six ways of accessing the intrinsic nature are unsurpassed because they access (1) the characteristics, (2) the basis, (3) ascertainment, (4) contact, (5) recollection, and (6) having become of the identity of that.**

These six ways of accessing the intrinsic nature are unsurpassed since those who fully understand these six topics will be able to comprehend with ease the entire range of qualities associated with complete purification. And what are these six? They consist of (1) the knowledge of the characteristics of the intrinsic nature; (2) the very basis, or ground, for their arising, or alternatively, the basis for continually abiding in the observation of the intrinsic nature; (3) the ascertainment of the intrinsic nature; (4) coming into direct contact with this nature in actuality; (5) recollecting it again and again; and (6) arriving at the identity of this intrinsic nature, or reaching the culmination of thorough establishment.

Second is the explanation of each of these six topics according to the meaning of the headings.

Characteristics

Concerning the first topic, characteristics, the treatise states:

> **The characteristics are just as in the summary.**

> **The characteristics are** [those of] suchness, in which there are no distinctions between an apprehended and apprehender, nor between something expressed and something that expresses it. This is **just as** was taught **in the summary.**

The characteristics of the intrinsic nature, complete purification, were taught in the summary above, where it was shown that suchness is free of four factors, such as an apprehended. Thus, these characteristics can be understood in precisely the manner that they were taught in that context.

The Basis

Concerning the second topic, the treatise states:

> The basis is all phenomena
> And all the sublime words of the sūtras.

> **The basis is** form and **all** other **phenomena and all the sub-
> lime words of the sūtras,** such as proclamations in song. These
> two are presented in terms of thorough affliction and com-
> plete purification.

The "basis" [for the intrinsic nature] is held to be the subject matter,
referring to all the phenomena that comprise thorough affliction and
complete purification, and the expressions used to convey this subject
matter, meaning all the collections of sūtra, which consist of the twelve
divisions of the Buddha's sublime words.

Why is it that these are considered the basis for the intrinsic nature? Phenomena are held to be the basis because the transcendence
of suffering is attained by ascertaining all phenomena in terms of con-
vention as those which should be embraced, avoided, and so on, and
in terms of the ultimate as being beyond observation. The Buddha's
sublime words are also held to be the basis because it is by engaging in
study and contemplation of these teachings that one eliminates ignorance concerning the manner in which one should practice the path.

ASCERTAINMENT

Concerning the third topic, the treatise states:

> The ascertainment of that
> Refers to the correct way of directing the mind
> Based on the sūtras of the Great Vehicle,
> Which constitutes the entire path of joining.

> **The ascertainment of that refers to the correct way of direct-
> ing the mind based on the sūtras of the Great Vehicle, which
> constitutes the entire path of joining** as delineated in terms of
> study, reflection, and meditation.

Ascertainment of this meaning is explained to entail the entirety of the path of joining, which consists of directing one's mind in the correct manner in reliance upon the intended meaning of the Great Vehicle's sūtras.

Why is this referred to as "ascertainment"? It is referred to as such because one ascertains, or recognizes, the meaning of the intrinsic nature by directing one's mind [to this meaning] on the paths of accumulation and joining, utilizing the three forms of insight as spelled out in the sūtras.

CONTACT

Concerning the fourth topic, the treatise states:

> **Because the authentic view has been attained,**
> **Contact occurs when suchness is attained and**
> **   experienced**
> **By way of the direct perception**
> **Brought on by the path of seeing.**

> **Because the authentic view has been attained, contact occurs**
> **when suchness is attained and experienced by way of the di-**
> **rect perception brought on by the path of seeing.**

"Contact" occurs when the authentic, supramundane view is attained with the eye of insight, the subject. Through this accomplishment one attains and experiences the object, suchness, through the path of seeing. Divested of those stains that are eliminated through seeing, suchness is attained in actuality by way of direct perception during meditative equipoise and experienced via the authentic view in the ensuing attainment.

RECOLLECTION

Concerning the fifth topic, the treatise states:

Recollection is the path of meditating on
The nature that was seen with awareness.
Constituted by the aspects of enlightenment,
This serves to eliminate the stains.

Recollection is the path of meditating on the nature that was seen with awareness. Constituted by the aspects of enlightenment, this serves to eliminate the stains. Thus, "recollection" is explained to serve the purpose of eradicating the residual stains that are characterized by being eliminated by meditating on suchness.

Recollection involves repeatedly recalling and realizing, in the context of the path of cultivation, what was realized when the intrinsic nature was directly seen with individual, self-awareness at the prior stage. In this way, the term "recollection" refers to all that constitutes the factors of enlightenment. The path of cultivation is [referred to as such] because it involves eradicating those stains that are eliminated through cultivation.

IDENTIFICATION

The sixth topic contains two further divisions: (1) an identification of the essence of the final, fundamental transformation and (2) a detailed explanation of its unique features.

AN IDENTIFICATION OF THE ESSENCE OF THE FINAL, FUNDAMENTAL TRANSFORMATION

On the first topic, the treatise states:

Arriving at the identity of that
Refers to suchness divested of stains,
Where all appears simply as suchness.
This is also the establishment
Of fundamental transformation.

Arriving at the identity of that refers to suchness divested of stains, where all appears simply as suchness because the path of cultivation has removed all remaining stains, thereby divesting suchness of stains. Once this has taken place, all that appears is, by virtue of the final path, simply suchness. "Arriving at the identity of that" is, thus, when the object is simply that. **This is also the** thorough **establishment of fundamental transformation.**

To arrive at the identity of suchness, the way all phenomena truly are, refers to suchness being divested of all adventitious stains. Once this has taken place, the way things appear completely matches the way they actually are. In other words, all phenomena appear as nothing but suchness. Moreover, at this time, fundamental transformation has reached a point of completion. Though this fundamental transformation is indeed present from the first ground onward, on this final ground this transformation is final and complete.

The Unique Features of Fundamental Transformation

This section is further divided into (1) a summary and (2) a detailed explanation.

A Summary

On the first topic, the treatise states:

> This tenfold way of accessing
> The fundamental transformation
> Is unsurpassable because one
> Accesses the essence,
> Substance, individuals, distinct features,
> Requirements, basis, directing the mind,
> Application, flaws, and benefits.

It may be asked, "How is one to access this fundamental transformation and do so in an unsurpassable manner?"

This tenfold way of accessing the fundamental transformation is unsurpassable because one accesses (1) the essence,
(2) substance, (3) individuals, (4) distinct features, (5) requirements, (6) basis, (7) directing the mind, (8) application, (9)
flaws, and (10) benefits.

There are ten topics whereby one may come to understand this fundamental transformation and access it through practice. This way of accessing it is unsurpassable insofar as these ten enable one to thoroughly
comprehend the nature of this transformation in a precise manner
and, by putting this understanding into practice, attain the final result.

What are these ten topics? They are (1) its nature or essence, (2) its
entity or substance, (3) individuals, (4) distinct features, (5) requirements, (6) basis or support, (7) directing the mind, (8) application, (9)
flaws, and (10) benefits.

A Detailed Explanation of the Ten Topics

Second is a detailed explanation that matches the preceding summary.

Essence

Concerning the first topic, the treatise states:

> Accessing the essence
> Refers to suchness devoid of stains,
> As the adventitious stains and suchness
> Do not appear and appear.

Accessing the essence, or nature, of the fundamental transformation refers to suchness devoid of stains, as the adventitious stains and suchness do not appear and appear, respectively. Thus, the nature of this fundamental transformation is
presented.

Accessing the nature, or essence, of this fundamental transformation refers to suchness, the intrinsic nature, devoid of adventitious stains, meaning that these adventitious stains and suchness do not and do appear, respectively. Hence, the intrinsic nature appears as it is in essence: devoid of stains.

Substance

On the second topic, the treatise states:

> Accessing substantial entities involves
> The transformation of the shared awareness
> Of the environment into suchness,
> The transformation of the sūtras' basic field
> Of phenomena into suchness,
> And the transformation
> Of the unshared awareness of the realm
> Of sentient beings into suchness.

> Accessing substantial entities involves (1) the complete transformation of the shared awareness of the environment into suchness, (2) the complete transformation of the sūtras' basic field of phenomena into suchness, and (3) the complete transformation of the unshared awareness of the realm of sentient beings into suchness. Thus, the entities [that undergo] fundamental transformation are involved in a fundamental transformation into three types of suchness. There are also three different fruitions that ensue in relation to these three. These fruitions are those of appearance, instruction, and complete revelation.

Accessing the entities or substance of this complete and fundamental transformation is taught, in the present context, in terms of three categories. First is the complete and fundamental transformation into suchness of the awareness, or perceptions, of the external universe, which appear as though they were shared. Second is the transformation into suchness of that which expresses, the appearances of names, words, and letters in the sūtras' basic field of phenomena. Third is the fundamental transformation into suchness of the minds and mental events—the collections of awareness—of the realm of sentient beings, which comprise distinct mind streams that are not shared.

There are no phenomena whatsoever that are not included in the basic field of phenomena. Therefore, when this fundamental transformation takes place, there is an inconceivable range of qualities within the undefiled basic field, corresponding to the totality of subjects in all their variety.

Nevertheless, here [they are presented in terms of] the attainment of the three bodies. The extension of suchness without limitation—in which everything that appears as the environment and, by extension, the body, undergoes a fundamental transformation—is the attainment of the body of qualities. Second, the mastery of the uninterrupted and inexhaustible qualities of the melodious sound of the Dharma—the fundamental transformation of all the conditioned verbal factors exemplified by the sūtras—is the attainment of the body of complete enjoyment. The fundamental transformation of all that comprises the mind—the all-ground and the seven collections of consciousness that depend upon it—is the attainment of the emanation body and its attendant knowledge of the five wakefulnesses. Alternatively, these may be viewed, respectively, as the completely pure appearance of the realms and bodies, the teaching of the sacred Dharma, and the revelation of all domains of knowledge through the wakefulness that knows things as they are and in their multiplicity.

That which comprises the embodied, along with verbal sounds, may appear in a shared manner prior to this fundamental transformation. The mind, by contrast, is not shared. When fundamental transformation takes place, however, all phenomena appear as suchness. Since there is nothing apart from this suchness, and nothing impure remains, we may draw a distinction in terms of there being nothing but pure self-appearance. Nevertheless, while such appearances do occur, from the perspective of those who have yet to undergo this fundamental transformation suchness will continue to manifest in a differentiated manner, in terms of a distinct teacher and teaching, for example.

INDIVIDUALS

On the third topic, the treatise states:

> As for accessing individuals,
> The first two are the complete
> Transformation of suchness
> For bodhisattvas and buddhas.
> The last also pertains
> To listeners and self-realized buddhas.

As for accessing individuals, the first two fruitions of the fundamental transformation into suchness **are** unshared in the sense of being **the complete transformation of suchness for bodhisattvas and buddhas,** respectively. Because **the last** fundamental transformation **also pertains to listeners and self-realized buddhas,** it is shared.

When it comes to accessing the fundamental transformation as it pertains to certain individuals, the first two forms of fundamental transformation that were described above are complete and fundamental transformations into suchness that are taken as objects by buddhas and bodhisattvas, respectively. In terms of the three kāyas, the body of qualities is the object of a buddha, while the body of perfect enjoyment is the object of the bodhisattvas. The reason for this is that the buddhas and bodhisattvas have mastery over the limitless appearances of the sacred Dharma, pure realms, and completely pure bodies, while the listeners do not.

The latter transformation is the fundamental transformation of the mind, which pertains to the listeners and solitary buddhas as well. How so? In terms of the three kāyas, the listeners and solitary buddhas are able to see the emanation body, with its all-encompassing wakefulness. Alternatively, we may say that they have undergone the latter fundamental transformation in a merely partial manner, insofar as theirs is a fundamental transformation of the afflicted consciousness that is based upon their all-ground. Hence, while it does seem to be taught that the latter fundamental transformation is common to all four types of noble beings, the fundamental transformation of the mind experienced by the listeners and solitary buddhas is incomplete.

DISTINCT FEATURES

On the fourth topic, the treatise states:

> **Accessing its distinct features involves**
> **The distinct feature of the completely pure realms**
> **Of the buddhas and bodhisattvas,**
> **As well as, due to the attainment of the body of qualities,**
> **The body of perfect enjoyment and the emanation body,**
> **And vision, instruction, and mastery.**
> **These are the distinct features in terms of attainment.**

Accessing its distinct features involves the distinct feature of the completely pure realms of the buddhas and bodhisattvas, as well as, due to the attainment of the body of qualities, the body of perfect enjoyment and the emanation body, respectively, **and** the **vision** of all objects of cognition, **instruction** in the form of wondrous and inconceivable entrances to the vast and profound, **and mastery** in accomplishing the welfare of others. **These are the distinct features in terms of attainment.**

Accessing the distinct features of this complete and fundamental transformation refers to the fundamental transformation of the buddhas and bodhisattvas. How is this brought about? This final fundamental transformation is brought about through the power of the nonconceptual wakefulness that thoroughly realizes the twofold absence of self. And what is this like? All phenomena appear as the nature of a thorough and total fundamental transformation, complete enlightenment, or transcendence of suffering.

The completely pure realms that extend throughout the reaches of space are a distinct feature of this fundamental transformation. Likewise, in attaining the body of qualities, body of perfect enjoyment, and emanation body, respectively, one has pure wakefulness that beholds all phenomena, teaches the wondrous profound and vast Dharma of the Great Vehicle and, through the attainment of the unobstructed power of superknowledge and other such factors, one has complete mastery in benefiting others in line with one's commitment. These are the distinct features of their attainment, which is superior to that of the listeners and solitary buddhas.

REQUIREMENTS

On the fifth topic, the treatise states:

> **Accessing the realization of the requirements**
> **Refers to distinct past aspirations,**
> **The distinct focal point**
> **Of the revelation of the Great Vehicle,**
> **And the distinct thorough application to the ten grounds.**

> Concerning **accessing the realization of the requirements,** the fundamental and complete transformation achieved by the bodhisattvas is distinctly superior to that of the listeners and the self-realized buddhas in three ways. This **refers to** their **distinct past aspirations,** as they aspire to attain complete enlightenment, **the distinct focal point of** the sublime words of **the revelation of the Great Vehicle, and the distinct thorough application to** cultivating the remedies of the obscurations in order to reach **the ten grounds.**

Accessing the realization, or understanding, of those factors that are requirements, or prerequisites, to this extraordinary fundamental and complete transformation refers to the following. First are the distinct aspirations that one makes with the wish to attain great, unsurpassed enlightenment. Such past aspirations include the ten great aspirations of the bodhisattvas. Next is the distinction of eliminating superimpositions concerning the topic of the two truths, which comes about by focusing on the entire range of the Buddha's profound and vast sublime words, which reveal the path and fruition of the Great Vehicle. Third is the distinct application as one proceeds through the ten grounds in order to bring the process of abandonment and realization to a point of culmination. It must be understood that these three distinctions are the causes of this final fundamental transformation, which is superior to that of the listeners and solitary buddhas. These are its distinct requirements.

BASIS

The discussion of the support contains both a summary and a detailed explanation. Concerning the first, the treatise states:

> **Accessing the basis, or support,**
> **Involves a sixfold access**
> **To nonconceptual wakefulness**
> **Because one accesses the focal point,**
> **The relinquishment of marks,**
> **Authentic application, characteristics,**
> **Benefits, and complete understanding.**

> **Accessing the basis, or support,** of this fundamental transformation **involves a sixfold access to nonconceptual wakefulness because one accesses** (1) **the focal point,** (2) **the relinquishment of marks,** (3) **authentic application,** (4) **characteristics,** (5) **benefits,** and (6) **complete understanding.**

To access the basis, support, or foundation of this final, complete, and fundamental transformation is to enter into nonconceptual wakefulness. Why? Because to attain this fundamental transformation one must actualize suchness, the primordial purity that is the way things truly are, and access the nature of this suchness. This, in turn, is brought about by the nonconceptual wakefulness that realizes suchness as it is. Without such wakefulness such a fundamental transformation will never be attained. It is, therefore, the support of this fundamental transformation.

What is nonconceptual wakefulness? There are six points that enable one to come to a full and unmistaken understanding of this principle: (1) accessing the focal points that allow one to generate this wakefulness; (2) relinquishment of the characteristics that conflict with it; (3) the authentic application to the process that arouses this wakefulness in one's mind stream; (4) the characteristics of the functioning or experiential domain of this wakefulness; (5) the benefits derived from it; and (6) a complete understanding of the very essence of this wakefulness.

Second is an explanation of the six topics outlined in the preceding summary.

The Focal Points

Concerning the first topic, the treatise states:

> **First, accessing the focal point**
> **Should be understood to involve four points:**
> **The teacher of the Great Vehicle,**
> **Interest in and certainty about it,**
> **And completion of the accumulations.**

> **First, accessing the focal point** of nonconceptual wakefulness **should be understood to involve four points:** (1) devotion to one's spiritual friend, **the teacher of the Great Vehicle,** (2) **interest in** the Great Vehicle, (3) **certainty about it, and** (4) **completion of the accumulations** for the sake of enlightenment. If any one of these is missing, nonconceptual wakefulness will not arise.

Accessing the focal points can be understood to be a fourfold process. To develop nonconceptual wakefulness one must focus on the vast and profound scriptures that teach the Great Vehicle. One must also listen to, and develop supreme conviction in, the unmistaken practical instructions by serving a spiritual guide of the Great Vehicle. Furthermore, one must develop certainty free from doubts in the meaning of these instructions by relying on the four forms of reasoning and completely perfect the accumulations by directing the mind in accord with the definite meaning. Since nonconceptual wakefulness will not arise in the correct manner if even one of these focal points is absent, one is advised to practice in the manner described here.

RELINQUISHMENT OF MARKS

On the second topic, the treatise states:

> **Second, accessing the relinquishment of marks**
> **Involves four points as well.**
> **One relinquishes the marks**
> **Of the discordant, remedies,**
> **Suchness, and realization.**
> **This brings about, in progression,**
> **The complete relinquishment of marks**
> **That are coarse, intermediate, subtle,**
> **And connected for an extended duration.**

Second, accessing the relinquishment of marks involves four points as well. One relinquishes (1) **the marks of the discordant** factors, such as desire, (2) the marks of **remedies** like repulsiveness, (3) the effort involved in contemplating **suchness, and** (4) the marks of the **realization** brought about by training on the grounds. **This brings about, in progression, the complete relinquishment of marks that are** (1) **coarse** because they cause negative tendencies and are easy to realize, (2) **intermediate** because they remedy [negative tendencies], (3) **subtle** because they are the remedy for everything else, **and** (4) **connected** [to the mind stream] **for an extended duration** because they result from training.

Second, accessing the relinquishment of the marks of the conceited mind also involves four factors: (1) abandoning the mark of fixating on discordant factors such as desire; (2) abandoning the mark of fixating on repulsiveness and the other remedies that eliminate these discordant factors; (3) abandoning the mark of fixating on the focal point of suchness; and (4) abandoning the mark of fixating on the qualities of realization, such as the ten strengths, the subject that realizes, or the authentic view that results from treading the path. These are all concepts that conflict with wakefulness. Relinquishing them brings about the attainment of wakefulness in its purest form.

As taught in the *Sūtra That Teaches the Dhāraṇī of Nonconceptuality*, relinquishing the four marks outlined above brings about a concurrent relinquishment of those marks that are coarse, intermediate, and subtle, up to those marks that remain associated with one's mind stream for a long time and which are difficult to discard. Because afflictive phenomena like attachment, which cause negative tendencies, are easy to understand and abandon, the coarse marks of fixating on these discordant factors is relinquished first. The next relinquishment concerns the intermediate marks that ensue from seeing their remedies, such as repulsiveness, as something positive. Suchness is the unsurpassed remedy for all that needs to be eliminated and also the most sublime factor that is to be realized. For these reasons relinquishing the subtle concepts of fixating on suchness and clinging to it as a mark is very difficult. Hence, it is relinquished after the preceding factors. The mark of fixating on realization itself is relinquished after all others. Since the subtle aspiration that involves desiring to attain a higher level of realization is not surrendered in the context of the grounds and paths, association with these marks persists for a long time. Until nonconceptual wakefulness has completely matured, it remains linked with the mind stream in the form of subtle thinking.

AUTHENTIC APPLICATION

On the third topic, the treatise states:

> **Accessing authentic application**
> **Likewise contains four points:**
> **Application with a focal point,**
> **Application without a focal point,**

> Application without focusing on a focal point,
> And the application of focusing on the absence of a focal
> point.

Accessing authentic application likewise contains four points: (1) **application with** mere awareness as one's **focal point**, (2) **application without** taking an object as one's **focal point**, (3) **application without focusing on a focal point** (because awareness itself is not feasible in the absence of an object of awareness), **and** (4) **the application of focusing on** nonduality, **the absence of** the **focal point** of duality.

Authentic application also involves four points. In the first application one observes that all phenomena are nothing more than mind. Based on that, one's application is such that the apprehended is not observed. This then leads to an application in which neither apprehended nor apprehender are observed. Based upon that, one's subsequent application involves the observation of suchness, without observing any apprehended or apprehender at all. This approach enables one to generate nonconceptual wakefulness.

While it is easy to realize that external objects are devoid of nature, the nonobservation of the mind that apprehends them is more difficult. The same can be said of the remaining steps in this progression. Thus, these are produced in the mind stream in a step-by-step manner in a similar manner to the account of heat being the meditative absorption of the attainment of appearance and so forth [in terms of the stages on the path of joining].

CHARACTERISTICS

On the fourth topic, the treatise states:

> Accessing the characteristics
> Must be understood in terms of three points.
> In terms of abidance in the intrinsic nature,
> There is no duality, but abidance

Within the inexpressible intrinsic nature.
In terms of the absence of appearance,
There is no appearance of the two,
Of that which is expressed,
Of the faculties, of objects, of awareness,
And of the world of the environment.
As this is the case, this is declared not conceivable,
Not demonstrable, not present,
Not appearance, not awareness,
And not an abode.
This is how the characteristics of nonconceptual wakefulness
Are presented in the sūtras.
In terms of appearance, all phenomena
Appear equal to the center of space.
All that is conditioned
Appears like illusions and so on.

Accessing the characteristics of nonconceptual wakefulness must be understood in terms of three points. (1) In terms of abidance in the intrinsic nature, there is no duality of apprehended and apprehender, but abidance within the inexpressible intrinsic nature. (2) In terms of the absence of appearance, there is no appearance of the two, apprehended and apprehender, of that which is expressed by the mind, of the faculties, of objects, of awareness, and of the world of the environment.

At this point, one may ask, "Well, what is this meant to demonstrate?"

As this is the case, this is declared to be not conceivable as the dual entities of apprehended and apprehender, not demonstrable through expressions, not present in the form faculties of the eye and so forth, not form or another such appearance, not awareness (since this is not an awareness [of anything]), and not an abode (since there is no appearance of the entities of the environment). This is how the characteristics of nonconceptual wakefulness are presented in the sūtras. (3) In

terms of appearance, the demonstration of the characteristics of wakefulness, **all phenomena appear equal to the center of space** because all marks of their respective subjects have been relinquished. Therefore, **all that is conditioned appears** as unreal, **like illusions,** mirages, dreams, **and so on.**

Accessing the characteristics of nonconceptual wakefulness can be understood in terms of three points: (1) the characteristic of abiding in the essence of the intrinsic nature, (2) the characteristic of settling into [nonconceptual wakefulness] where there are no appearances, and (3) the characteristic of settling into [nonconceptual wakefulness] where there are appearances.

Concerning the first of these, when abiding in suchness, the intrinsic nature of all phenomena, the duality of apprehender and apprehended (or, alternatively, the conceptual division between the two truths) is absent. Fully abiding in the intrinsic nature is also ineffable insofar as it cannot be expressed verbally via limited concepts or marks. This reaches a point of culmination in the wakefulness of the buddhas, in which the two truths are realized to be inseparable and of one taste. This wakefulness sees the intrinsic nature as it is, whereas an approximation is seen on the path of training.

The second point concerns the attainment of nonconceptual wakefulness where appearances are absent. This includes the dualistic appearance of apprehended and apprehender associated with the nonconceptual sense consciousnesses; the expressions that correspond with these dualistic appearances, which are formulated by the conceptual mind that fixates on them (this is an internal expression or, said differently, the mind's conceptualization of apprehended and apprehender); the eyes and other internal sense faculties; form and other external objects; the eye consciousness and other forms of awareness; and the commonly experienced world of the environment. Since all of these have completely subsided and are entirely absent, there are no differentiations whatsoever in suchness, which appears to be of one taste. This is referred to as "the subsiding of dualistic appearances into emptiness."

Therefore, the aforementioned six topics refer, respectively, to (1) the absence of conception related to visual and other sense consciousnesses, (2) the absence of verbal description, (3) the absence of basis or support for the arising of consciousness, (4) the absence of the appearance of objects, (5) the absence of subjective awareness, and (6) the absence of a place, meaning an environment that serves as a commonly experienced support. These principles demonstrate the characteristics of nonconceptual wakefulness and are taught in accordance with the presentation given by the Tathāgata in the sūtras. *The Prophecy Requested by Kāśyapa* from the *Ratnakūṭa* states:

> Kāśyapa, permanence is one extreme and impermanence is a second. The middle that lies between these two extremes is the absence of analysis, the absence of description, the absence of support, the absence of appearance, the absence of awareness, and the absence of place. Kāśyapa, this middle way is referred to as "the genuine, individual discernment of phenomena."

This teaching also applies to self and no self, cyclic existence and the transcendence of suffering, existence and nonexistence, and so on. The middle way that lies between these polarities is, as was taught above, devoid of analysis, etc.

Hence, wakefulness devoid of appearances is beyond the nature of appearances. Naturally luminous and equal to space, this is referred to as "nonconceptual wakefulness devoid of appearance." In essence, this wakefulness transcends consciousness and cannot be categorized as being conditioned, unconditioned, or as any other factor. For these reasons, the essence of this wakefulness is not restricted to any such appearance. Indeed, it is naturally luminous and inseparable from the intrinsic nature.

In relation to the wakefulness that realizes the way things are, we may also want to distinguish the wakefulness that realizes things in their multiplicity, which sees all appearances as equal yet distinct, while never wavering from this basic state. Without any conflict between them, these two forms of wakefulness combine as unity. How is this so? Within the state of suchness—the intrinsic nature—all phenomena are of one taste. Nevertheless, without any wavering from this state, all subjects simply appear. Hence, there is no contradiction between these two, because while appearances do manifest unceasingly to the self-appearance of the wakefulness that beholds the intrinsic nature, there is no fixation on them as this and that. From this perspective, the absence of appearances taught above is perfectly complete since here one has moved beyond the nature of ordinary dualistic perception and other such factors. This incredibly important and profound topic has been discussed here as a supplementary explanation.

Third, in terms of appearance, during the meditative equipoise all phenomena are of one taste and remain undifferentiable in terms of their essential suchness. In other words, they appear as equality, which can be likened to the center of space. The wakefulness that is attained subsequent to this equipoise, on the other hand, may perceive the entire range of conditioned phenomena, which appear like illusions, optical illusions, dreams, and other such appearances that lack any nature of their own.

On the ground of buddhahood this process culminates in a realization within which there is no equipoise or subsequent attainment as distinct from the other. An approximation of this realization occurs on the grounds of the noble ones, whereas on the path of mantra something that resembles it already arises in the mind stream with the occurrence of the symbolic wakefulness due to the profound skillful means of this path.

In this way it must be understood that while the perfected way that a buddha sees things involves two forms of wakefulness (the wakefulness that sees things as they are and the wakefulness that sees things in their multiplicity), and while the meditative equipoise of the path of training may or may not involve appearance, there is no contradiction in either of these cases. This is a vital point to comprehend. Hence, due to the importance of this topic, I have offered this explanation along with a bit of supplementary discussion.

BENEFITS

On the fifth topic, the treatise states:

Accessing the benefits involves four points:
The attainment of the perfection of the body of qualities,
The attainment of unexcelled bliss,
The attainment of the mastery of vision,
And the attainment of the mastery of teaching.

Accessing the benefits involves four points: (1) **the attainment of** the fundamental transformation through **the perfection of the body of qualities,** (2) **the attainment of** supreme, **unexcelled bliss** through which defiling bliss is relinquished, (3) **the attainment of the mastery of vision** through which the objects of knowledge are realized as they are and in their multiplicity, **and** (4) **the attainment of the mastery of teaching,** which brings about numerous gateways that are taught in a fitting manner.

Fifth, accessing the benefits of nonconceptual wakefulness involves four points. Nonconceptual wakefulness itself brings about the attainment of the complete body of qualities, the culmination of the fundamental transformation in which one is divested of the two obscurations. Transcending ephemeral, unstable, and defiling bliss, along with its associated habitual tendencies, one attains unexcelled, great bliss, which is eternally immutable and not defiling. One attains mastery over pure and spontaneously present vision, which beholds all objects of cognition, as they are and in their multiplicity, in an unerring manner. Finally, one also attains mastery over [the ability] to teach the limitless beings in need of guidance. Without any effort one is able to teach them the various gateways to the Dharma—the principles of the profound and the vast—in a way that matches their individual interests.

From this perspective we can see that the cause of bringing about the culmination of the process of abandonment and realization is nonconceptual wakefulness itself, which is why these four benefits of wakefulness have been outlined here.

COMPLETE UNDERSTANDING

On the sixth topic, the treatise states:

> Accessing complete understanding
> Should be understood to be fourfold:
> Complete understanding of the remedy,
> Complete understanding of the characteristics,
> Complete understanding of the distinctions,
> And complete understanding of the five functions.

Accessing complete understanding should be understood to be fourfold: (1) **complete understanding of the remedy** for the five discordant factors, (2) **complete understanding of the characteristics** of freedom from the five types of nonconceptuality, (3) **complete understanding of the** five superior **distinctions, and** (4) **complete understanding of the five functions** of wakefulness.

Sixth, accessing the complete understanding of the principle of wakefulness contains (1) a summary and (2) a detailed explanation. Concerning the first, accessing complete understanding can be understood to be fourfold: (1) complete understanding of the way in which wakefulness serves as a remedy for the discordant factors, (2) complete understanding of the characteristics by divesting oneself of the five forms of nonconceptuality that can lead one astray, (3) complete understanding of the five qualities that set it apart from inferior paths, and (4) complete understanding of the five functions of wakefulness.

Second, for the detailed explanation, we shall discuss the aforementioned four topics.

Remedies

On the first topic, the treatise states:

> Here nonconceptual wakefulness
> Should be understood to be the remedy
> For the apprehension of phenomena and persons,

Complete change, difference,
And denigration—
There are five apprehensions of the nonexistent
For which it is taught to be the remedy.

Here nonconceptual wakefulness should be fully understood
to be the remedy for the apprehension of nonexistent phenomena and nonexistent persons, for complete change (the
arising and so forth of that which does not exist), for the perceived difference between nonexistent phenomena and their
intrinsic nature, and for the denigration of taking phenomena
and persons that exist as products of the imagination to be
[completely] nonexistent. There are five apprehensions of the
nonexistent for which it is taught to be the remedy.

First is the knowledge of the remedies for the discordant factors. Since
nonconceptual wakefulness has entered into suchness without exag-
gerating or depreciating the way things are, meaning the inseparable
two truths, it eliminates all negative views that adhere to extreme positions. There are five such positions: (1) the belief in form and other
phenomena, (2) the belief in the self of persons, (3) the belief in arising
and cessation, meaning the complete transformation of things from an
earlier state, (4) the belief that phenomena and their intrinsic nature
are separate from one another, and (5) the belief that denigrates phenomena that are mere appearances by holding that they do not even
exist at the conventional level. These five have no bearing on the way
things are, and so lack establishment. Nevertheless, the ignorant in-
tellect believes in the two selves, arising and cessation, difference, and
denigration. Since all of these are involved with something that is not
the case, they are referred to as "belief in the nonexistent."

Nonconceptual wakefulness is itself taught to be the remedy for
these five distorted beliefs in that which does not exist. The entire
range of negative views, as exemplified by these four distorted views
that exaggerate and one distorted view that denigrates, will not occur
to those in possession of this nonconceptual wakefulness.

COMPLETE KNOWLEDGE OF THE CHARACTERISTICS

On the second topic, the treatise states:

> As for the complete knowledge of the characteristics,
> There is no directing of the mind, complete transcendence,
> Thorough pacification, the state of the essence,
> And apprehension of manifest signs.
> The specific characteristic is the abandonment of these five.

> **As for the complete knowledge of the characteristics, there
> is** (1) **no directing of the mind,** as in the case of a small child;
> (2) **complete transcendence** of concept and discernment,
> as in the second concentration and so forth; (3) **thorough
> pacification** of concepts, as is the case when one falls asleep,
> loses consciousness, and so forth; (4) **the state of the** noncon-
> ceptual **essence** of the eyes and so forth; **and** (5) the **appre-
> hension of manifest signs** involved when one entertains the
> thought, "I shall not think." **The specific characteristic is the
> abandonment of these five.**

Second, complete understanding of the characteristics of nonconceptual wakefulness is taught in terms of eliminating the five deviations
that are not in harmony with nonconceptual wakefulness. This is because while nonconceptual wakefulness does not see or grasp any image whatsoever that could serve as a focal object, it nevertheless does
see the suchness of all phenomena. [Such a mode of cognition is just
as unfathomable to an ordinary individual] as visual form is to a blind
person.

Wakefulness cannot be immediately demonstrated in an affirma-
tive manner to those whose perspective is limited in scope. In essence
it is entirely nonconceptual, meaning that it unerringly realizes the
fact that the intrinsic nature cannot be observed in relation to any
extreme position whatsoever. With this realization there is no fixation
at all, which is in harmony with the intrinsic nature.

Moreover, this is not nonconceptual in the sense of being unconscious, blocking consciousness, and so on. In other words, "nonconceptual" does not refer to simply not engaging the mind with mundane, conventional concepts that mix up words and their meanings. Likewise, though there are no such conceptual processes at work in the mind streams of newborn children or calves, such states are not referred to as "nonconceptuality." Though we may say that small children possess the mental capacity to mix words and their meanings, this associative apprehension is not active from birth, for they do not know how to engage in the process of conceptual discernment. It is the latter's state of mind that is taken as the example in the present context.

The mere transcendence of all forms of coarse and subtle conceptual activity, as is found in the forms of consciousness on the second absorption and above, is not nonconceptual wakefulness. Similarly, the mere pacification of thought is not what is meant here either, as such states occur while in the states of deep sleep, having fallen unconscious, intoxication, and the equilibrium of cessation.

This is also the case with things that are essentially nonconceptual by their very nature. This includes form and other sensory objects, as well as the eye and other sense organs. Though all of these are essentially nonconceptual, insofar as they are material objects, they are not nonconceptual wakefulness.

Clinging to the notion "I will not think of anything whatsoever" is not nonconceptual wakefulness either, for by thinking "I will not think" with certainty and clarity, one has already formed concepts about this and that. Since such clear grasping itself involves clinging to marks, it is not nonconceptual.

The characteristics of nonconceptual wakefulness are thus explained by not conflating them with, and eliminating, the character of these five factors that may be referred to by the term "nonconceptual."

Thus, it must be understood that what we are referring to here is individual self-awareness, which does not form even the slightest extreme view or conceptual elaboration and in which the haze of doubt concerning the unobservable nature of the way things are is absent. Thus, when the light of self-aware wakefulness has dawned from within, one may refer to it as nonconceptual wakefulness.

COMPLETE KNOWLEDGE OF DISTINCTIONS

On the third topic, the treatise states:

> As for the complete knowledge of the distinctions,
> There is an absence of conceptualization,
> Absence of limitation,
> Absence of abiding, endurance,
> And the unsurpassable.
> These are the five distinctions.

> As for the complete knowledge of the distinctions, there is
> (1) **an absence of conceptualization** concerning the flaws and
> good qualities of existence and peace, respectively, (2) an **ab-
> sence of limitation** since the specific and general characteris-
> tics of the cognizable are taken as objects correctly, (3) **absence
> of abiding** in the extremes of existence and peace, (4) **endur-
> ance,** in the sense of not passing beyond suffering without
> remainder, **and** (5) **the unsurpassable** qualities. These are the
> **five distinctions.**

Third, there are five distinctions that set this wakefulness apart from
that of the listeners and solitary buddhas: (1) there is no conceiving
of cyclic existence as something to abandon and the transcendence of
suffering as something to accept; (2) abandonment and realization are
not partial, but fully complete; (3) one does not dwell in the extreme
of existence, nor in that of peace; (4) by virtue of the eternal essence
of the body of qualities, one remains perpetually in cyclic existence
to benefit others; and (5) since there is nothing superior to this, its
qualities are supreme and unexcelled. Because they conceive in terms
of cyclic existence versus the transcendence of suffering etc., these distinctions do not pertain to the listeners and solitary buddhas.

COMPLETE KNOWLEDGE OF THE FUNCTIONS

On the fourth topic, the treatise states:

Finally, concerning the complete knowledge of the functions,
One distances oneself from concepts;
Unsurpassable bliss is granted;
One is freed from the obscurations
Of affliction and cognition;
All the features of the objects of cognition
Are accessed through the wakefulness
Attained subsequently;
The buddha fields are purified,
Sentient beings are completely matured,
And omniscience itself
Is established and granted.
These are the five distinctions of the function.

Finally, concerning the complete knowledge of the functions of wakefulness, (1) **one distances oneself from** the causes of **concepts** due to having overcome the full emergence [of the habitual tendencies]; (2) **unsurpassable bliss is granted** due to realizing the objects of cognition, just as they are and in their multiplicity; (3) **one is freed from the obscurations of affliction and cognition** due to having completely overcome the subtle developers, including their habitual tendencies; (4) **all the features of the objects of cognition are accessed through the wakefulness attained subsequent** to nonconceptuality; and (5) **the buddha fields are** completely **purified, sentient beings are completely matured, and omniscience itself is established and granted. These are the five distinctions of the function.**

Fourth, the last of these four forms of complete understanding relates to the functions of nonconceptual wakefulness. One such function is that one distances oneself from the causes of conceptuality since one has conquered their emergence. This is the result of individual effort. It also bestows undefiling bliss, which is unexcelled in character, since one realizes all phenomena in an unerring manner and accomplishes perpetual and everlasting bliss. This is the dominant result. Wakefulness also divests one of the emotional and cognitive obscurations, as one conquers the subtle developers and their habitual tendencies. This is the result of separation. Subsequent to the attainment of nonconceptual wakefulness, wakefulness unerringly realizes the specific characteristics of phenomena. This wakefulness has unhindered access to all forms of knowledge. This is the result that resembles its cause. Finally, purifying buddha fields, completely maturing sentient beings, and establishing and perfecting the qualities of total omniscience in one's own mind stream and granting them to others, when considered a single function, are the result of maturation. These five are the distinct functions of nonconceptual wakefulness.

DIRECTING THE MIND

On the seventh topic, the treatise states:

> As for directing the mind,
> The person who wishes
> To enter nonconceptual wakefulness,
> That bodhisattva,
> Should direct the mind in the following way.
> Due to not knowing suchness,
> That which is not true is wholly imagined.
> The so-called "entirety of seeds"
> Causes the appearance of duality where there is none.
> The distinct continua are based on that.
> Accordingly, causes and effects
> Do appear, but do not exist.
> The appearance of that is not the appearance of the intrinsic nature.
> When that does not appear, the intrinsic nature appears.
> Directing the mind correctly in this way,
> The bodhisattva enters
> Into nonconceptual wakefulness.
> Observing in this way brings about the observation
> Of mere awareness without the observation of objects.

The absence of the observation of objects
Brings about the absence of the observation of mere
   awareness.
The absence of the observation of that
Allows access to an observation where these two are not
   different.
When no distinction between the two is observed,
This is nonconceptual wakefulness,
Beyond object and observation,
Because the absence of the observation of any mark
Is what distinguishes this.

As for directing the mind, the person who ardently wishes to
enter nonconceptual wakefulness, that bodhisattva, should
direct the mind in the following way. Due to not knowing
suchness, because of the habitual tendencies of the ignorance
that has been present since beginningless time, that which is
not true is wholly imagined by thought. The so-called "entirety of seeds," i.e., the all-ground consciousness, causes the
appearance of duality where there is none. The six engaged
cognitions that appear as separate and distinct continua are
based on that all-ground. Not knowing this is the cause of error.

Accordingly, causes and effects do appear, but, since they
do not actually exist in the way they appear, they do not exist. The appearance of that, meaning the nature of apprehended
and apprehender, is not the appearance of the intrinsic nature,
which is empty of duality. When that duality of apprehended
and apprehender does not appear, the intrinsic nature appears.
Convinced that this is the case, the bodhisattva directs his or
her mind. Thus, directing the mind correctly in this way, the
bodhisattva enters into nonconceptual wakefulness as included
in the path of joining.

Observing in this way, i.e., as was just explained, brings
about access to the observation of mere awareness alone, without the observation of external objects. The absence of the observation of objects brings about the absence of the observation

of mere awareness as well because there is no object to be aware of. **The absence of the observation of that** [mere awareness] **allows access to an observation where these two**, the apprehended and the apprehender, **are not different. When no distinction between these two is observed, this is nonconceptual wakefulness, beyond** any **object** in terms of the duality of apprehended and apprehender **and** beyond any **observation** by a corresponding subject, **because the absence of the observation of any mark is what distinguishes this** [nonconceptual wakefulness].

The seventh topic concerns the manner in which one directs the mind to the fundamental transformation. An individual who wishes to correctly access the support of nonconceptual wakefulness, meaning a bodhisattva, must direct his or her mind as follows. Lacking knowledge of suchness, the way all phenomena are, causes fictitious phenomena—the duality of apprehended and apprehender—to be imagined by the deluded mind. "The entirety of seeds" associated with these phenomena is known as "the all-ground consciousness," which functions as the cause of the nonexistent yet apparent duality of apprehended and apprehender. Like a dream, all the various phenomena manifest from this stream of consciousness, contaminated as it is by the habitual tendencies that have proliferated from time immemorial. The engaging consciousnesses that are supported by the all-ground are each characterized as distinct, as each appears to occur on its own, definitively apprehending its own respective object. This is also referred to as "mind stream."

Under the influence of the false imagination that which does not exist appears. That is to say, the all-ground, functioning as the cause, along with its result, meaning the seven collections of consciousness along with their respective objects, appear in this manner from the perspective of the deluded mind as the phenomena that comprise the dualistic appearance of apprehended and apprehender. Though nonexistent in actuality, like a mirage and other such examples, such appearances are nothing more than the mind's own false imagination.

It is taught that due to the appearance of apprehended and apprehender the intrinsic nature does not appear, while due to the nonappearance of these two the intrinsic nature does appear. To explain, under the influence of the false imagination sentient beings wander throughout cyclic existence, not seeing the intrinsic nature. Bodhisattvas, on the other hand, understand this and direct their minds appropriately, thereby accessing nonconceptual wakefulness for the first time. The power of thought brings about the appearance of cyclic existence; it has no other cause. Hence, when it comes to understanding thorough affliction, there is no vital point more profound than this. Furthermore, since dualistic appearances are not what they seem, they are nothing more than inaccurate concepts. Understanding this enables one to eliminate fixating on them as such and provides access to nonconceptual wakefulness. Thus, when it comes to the path that leads to complete purification, this vital point is exceedingly profound as well.

By growing familiar with the process of directing the mind and observing in the manner explained above, one will observe all phenomena as mere awareness, mere mind. With this, one no longer observes external objects as objects of fixation. Not observing such objects, in turn, leads to the nonobservation of the mere awareness that apprehends them as this and that as well. Due to the nonobservation of this apprehension, one comes to observe the fact that apprehended and apprehender cannot be differentiated from one another, that they are an inseparable suchness beyond all forms of thought and expression. This nonobservation of any phenomena that could be delineated as either apprehended or apprehender is what we refer to as "nonconceptual wakefulness," in which there is not even the slightest object to be observed and no subject to observe it. Consequently, one does not observe any marks whatsoever, such as those associated with apprehended and apprehender, and existence and nonexistence. Since nonconceptual wakefulness is distinguished in terms of this nonobservation, there is not even the slightest rationale for anything that would be considered conceptual.

APPLICATION

On the eighth topic, the treatise states:

Accessing the grounds through application
Should be known to involve four points:
Through the full application of interest
One accesses the grounds of inspired conduct,
The phase of ascertainment;
Through the full application of discerning realization
One accesses the first ground,
The phase of contact;
Through the full application by means of cultivation
One accesses the six impure grounds
And the three pure grounds,
The phase of recollection;
Through the application of perfection
One accesses the spontaneous accomplishment
Of uninterrupted buddha activity.
Therefore, this is the phase of
"Arriving at the identity of that."

Accessing the grounds through application should be known to involve four points: (1) through the full application of interest one accesses the grounds of inspired conduct, the phase of ascertainment that was described above; (2) through the full application of discerning realization one accesses the first ground, the full realization of the basic field of phenomena by way of the path of seeing—this is the phase of contact that was taught above; (3) through the full application by means of cultivation one accesses the six impure grounds, beginning with the second, upon which there is experience of marks, and the three completely pure grounds, beginning with the eighth, upon which there is spontaneous access to the absence of marks—this is the phase of recollection that was taught above; and (4) through the application of perfection one accesses the spontaneous accomplishment of uninterrupted buddha activity at the ground of buddhahood. Therefore, this is the phase of "arriving at the identity of that" that was taught above.

Eighth, practicing this wakefulness, meaning to exert oneself and apply oneself to it, provides access to the individual grounds or bases present at the various phases of the grounds and paths. This should be understood to involve four aspects. First, even though one has yet to directly realize the intrinsic nature, utilizing the three forms of insight and applying oneself to wakefulness with interest constitutes the application upon the grounds of inspired conduct. This phase encompasses the path of joining and involves an approximation of ascertainment.

The application of a thorough, discerning realization of the intrinsic nature, rather than as a mere abstract concept, provides access to the first ground, the phase in which one comes into direct contact with thatness.

Once thatness has been realized, the next application involves familiarizing oneself with it again and again. This provides access to the so-called "six impure grounds," which refers to the second to the seventh. This is a phase in which one is thoroughly involved with marks. The purification of this thorough involvement with marks provides access to the eighth through tenth grounds. These last nine grounds encompass the phase in which one recalls what has already been realized.

Applying oneself to the ground of perfection provides access to the effortless and spontaneously accomplished activities of buddhahood, which continue without interruption for so long as sentient beings remain throughout the reaches of space. This application takes place once one has reached, or arrived at, the identity of the intrinsic nature, having eliminated the two obscurations. It is immutable wakefulness, indivisible from the basic field.

FLAWS

On the ninth topic, the treatise states:

> Accessing the flaws
> Implies the four flaws that are
> Due to a lack of fundamental transformation:
> The flaw of lacking a support for not engaging affliction,
> The flaw of lacking a support for engaging the path,
> The flaw of lacking a basis for identifying

The individuals who have transcended suffering,
And the flaw of lacking a basis for recognizing
Three distinct types of enlightenment.

**Accessing the flaws implies the four flaws that are due to a
lack of fundamental transformation:** (1) **the flaw of lacking a
support**, in the form of the wakefulness that has relinquished
obscuration, **for not engaging affliction;** (2) **the flaw of lacking a support for engaging the path** that dispels obscuration;
(3) **the flaw of lacking a basis for identifying the individuals who have transcended suffering**, because such recognition
must be made based on their attainment of fundamental transformation; **and** (4) **the flaw of lacking a basis for recognizing
three distinct types of enlightenment**, because [such recognition must be made] based on the presence of fundamental transformation.

Ninth, accessing flaws refers to the four flaws related to the absence of
fundamental transformation. The first flaw is lacking a support that
will keep the afflictions from reengaging a mind stream that has already eliminated them. Second is the flaw of lacking a support for the
path that remedies the afflictions that engage the mind stream. Third is
the flaw of the absence of a basis for recognizing those individuals who
have transcended suffering. Finally, the fourth flaw is lacking a basis
for recognizing the three distinct types of enlightenment, meaning the
end result attained by the listeners, the solitary buddhas, and those
who practice the Great Vehicle.

Now let us go into more detail concerning the key points that one
should understand from this discussion. If, for instance, there were no fundamental transformation whereby one could eliminate the discards and
attain realization by virtue of the path, then a flaw would ensue in which
there would be no support that would keep the afflictions that were previously eliminated from reengaging that same mind stream. The discards
that are eliminated on the path of seeing, for example, do not recur in the
same mind stream once they have been eliminated due to the fact that the
mind stream of that bodhisattva will already have undergone a complete

and fundamental transformation. Indeed, there is no point at which they could do so. On the other hand, if the mind stream has not undergone this fundamental transformation, then obscurations that had already been eliminated at one point in time could recur just as before.

This is the case all the way up to buddhahood. A given mind stream that has yet to undergo a fundamental transformation serves as the support for engaging the discards that are to be eliminated. Once this fundamental transformation has taken place, however, this mind stream serves as a support for not engaging those same factors due to the power of the fundamental transformation.

"What is the problem," one may wonder, "if these discards, like burnt seeds, were simply to not recur once their seeds had been conquered, even in the absence of this so-called "fundamental transformation"?

In response, we may say that in such a case the seeds of the discards would indeed have been overcome, but this would have to be posited in relation to a specific mind stream. If a certain mind stream has given rise to the wakefulness that remedies the discards, it may be identified, for example, as a stream that has exhausted the defilements, but without referring [to a transformed mind stream] one could not understand how these seeds were overcome. For this very reason it is impermissible [to make such claims] without further specification.

From this perspective we can see that it is by virtue of the difference between the fundamental transformation of a mind stream divested of the seeds of the discards and its prior state that the discards do not recur. It is not that the mind stream ceases and, consequently, can no longer serve as a support. Hence, it is in some specific mind streams that the defilements arise and others in which they do not, which is due to the fact that some have undergone this fundamental transformation and others have not. This can be likened to eyes that are not afflicted with cataracts and which, consequently, do not witness the appearance of hairs.

Another flaw that ensues from the absence of this fundamental transformation is that there is no support for engaging the path that serves as the remedy for the discards. The support for a specific mind stream to access progressively higher [levels of attainment], as when a particular individual is on the path of seeing, that another is on the second ground, and so on, is the prior state of fundamental transformation [experienced by that mind stream]. Without such a prior state the occurrence of a subsequent state would be impossible, just as there can be no stem, nor any other part of a plant, if a seed has yet to sprout. The conventional labels associated with the various paths, along with their respective meanings, apply to the different fundamental transformations, as is the case when we refer to the ground of buddhahood as "the path of no more training."

Yet another flaw associated with the lack of this fundamental transformation is that there would be no basis for recognizing the transcendence of suffering. For example, taking the continuum of the defiled aggregates as a basis, one may identify someone as an individual within cyclic existence. Just so, the identification of someone as an individual who has transcended suffering is made on the basis of identifying the fundamental transformation in which defilements are no longer present. In the absence of such a fundamental transformation there would be no basis within the mere continuum of the mind and other factors that comprise the aggregates for identifying a given individual as someone who has transcended suffering, as would have been the case in the phase prior to fundamental transformation.

Furthermore, if this were the case, there would also be no basis for using the term "the transcendence of suffering" to identify an individual who has moved beyond suffering into the basic field without remainder, as is held to be the case on the paths of the listeners and solitary buddhas. Without a fundamental transformation such a term would be as baseless as talking about the horns of a rabbit.

"Even if there is no such basis, what is the problem?" one may object. "The mere cessation of what had previously been the aggregates is termed 'the transcendence of suffering,' just as one may say, 'there is no illness' when an illness has been cured."

In response we may say that if the aggregates that were previously present have definitively ceased and do not recur, then this itself implies their fundamental transformation. Hence, in this case there would also be fundamental transformation. Indeed, fundamental transformation is both the support and basis for identifying a given individual with the phrases "one who has transcended suffering" and "one who will no longer fall into cyclic existence." For this very reason it cannot be asserted that there is no fundamental transformation. If one were to do so, it would follow that there is no cessation of the continuum of the aggregates and no nonrecurrence of them either, precisely because both the support and basis for the application of these terms would be lacking.

The path of the Great Vehicle brings about a transcendence of suffering within the basic field in which there is no remainder of the defiled aggregates. Nevertheless, in this transcendence of suffering the continuity of the undefiled bodies and forms of wakefulness is unceasing. This being the case, it should go without saying that this is the very identity of the complete and fundamental transformation.

Furthermore, the three different forms of so-called "enlightenment" associated with each of the three vehicles derive from different forms of fundamental transformation. In some cases the obscurations have only been partially purified, while in others they may be completely purified. Though the different forms of enlightenment are posited in relation to such differences, in the absence of fundamental transformation there is no basis for identifying the three distinct forms of enlightenment as such. Indeed, there would be no basis for identifying which of the three different types of enlightenment would occur when one moves beyond suffering into the basic field without remainder. Hence, describing each type of enlightenment, such as explaining the magnitude of their respective qualities of abandonment and realization, would be as pointless as trying to explain whether the son of a barren woman is handsome or not.

I have offered this extensive explanation here due to the fact that this has not been explained in detail in either the Indian or Tibetan commentaries of the past. May it delight the wise!

Benefits

On the tenth topic, the treatise states:

> **Accessing the opposite, the benefits,**
> **Should be understood to involve four points.**

> **Accessing the opposite** of these flaws, **the benefits** that relate
> to the presence of fundamental transformation, **should be**
> **understood to involve four points.**

The tenth topic concerns accessing the benefits of having this fundamental transformation, which occur once the four flaws associated with its absence have been averted. The four beneficial qualities can be understood from the preceding topic. Though a specific mind stream may not cease, it does remain present with the identity of a complete and fundamental transformation from its earlier state. As this is the case, it serves as a support for the perpetual nonrecurrence of the afflictions, as a support for engaging the path, as a basis for identifying the transcendence of suffering, and as a basis for identifying and distinguishing the differences between the three different types of enlightenment, meaning the liberations brought about by each of the three vehicles.

From this perspective we can see that the wakefulness of this complete and fundamental transformation is the basis for identifying the enlightenment of liberation and the transcendence of suffering. It is the source of inexhaustible positive qualities, as well as the sublime support for accomplishing, in accordance with their wishes, the temporal and ultimate welfare of each and every being that fills the reaches of space. Knowing this, fortunate individuals should endeavor to accomplish this wakefulness.

CONCLUSION

On the third topic, the treatise states:

> The nonexistent phenomena that appear
> Are likened to illusions, dreams, and so forth.
> Fundamental transformation
> Is likened to space, gold, water, and so forth.

To gain conviction that the false imagination's appearances manifest yet do not exist, examples are given in the following way. **The nonexistent phenomena that appear** while not existing **are likened to illusions, dreams,** mirages, echoes, **and so forth.** As for the way that the fundamental transformation is not subject to change, it is said that **fundamental trans-**

formation is likened to naturally pure **space,** excellent **gold,** clear **water, and so forth.** Space is exclusively pure by nature, and when this is not realized it is simply due to its association with adventitious factors such as mist, whereas once free from such factors, it is [seen to be] pure. This is not as if something previously impure had become pure. Rather, the observation of purity simply emerges when the causes preventing that observation are gone. It is not that the observation of its purity makes us committed to space being subject to change.

The same can be said with respect to the examples of gold and water. The examples of gold and water are not [likened to this fundamental transformation] in consideration of their substance, but rather due to simply having similar qualities. The example of space, on the other hand, shows everything. The words "and so forth" should be understood to imply, for instance, a fabric that is cleansed by the removal of its stains and all other such examples.

Third is the conclusion, which presents the topics discussed earlier, meaning phenomena and their intrinsic nature, using various examples. The appearance of the phenomena of cyclic existence is simply due to the false imagination. These appearances are referred to as "nonexistent phenomena" because they appear while lacking any essence of their own. Illusions, dreams, the reflection of the moon in water, and other such cases are used to illustrate the appearance of these phenomena. They appear to the deluded perspective yet do not exist, just as each of these examples appears while lacking any essential existence of what it appears to be.

The complete and fundamental transformation into the intrinsic nature is likened to naturally pure space, excellent gold, clear water, the sun unobstructed by clouds, and other such examples. In terms of the way things are, all phenomena have been free from the duality of apprehended and apprehender, as well as all other forms of impurity, from the very beginning. Nevertheless, due to the power of delusion, the way things are is obscured and things appear to be impure. When this is the case, it is said that no fundamental transformation has taken place. The strength of eliminating these impurities via the path brings about a state of complete concordance between the way things appear and the way things are. This marks the attainment of the ultimate fundamental transformation.

"If the intrinsic nature is subject to change," one may object, "insofar as it is not fundamentally transformed in one period and is transformed in another, then would it not be the case that its nature could not be pure from the very beginning and that it is subject to change?"

Primordially pure space can temporarily be clouded by mist and other such factors, gold can be covered with mud, water can be filled with sediment, and the sun can be blocked by clouds. These and other such examples show how things can be obscured, yet without that which is obscured being tainted by that which obscures it. Moreover, when the character of that which is free from obscuration becomes manifest, it is not the case that something new has come into existence. Similarly, it must be understood that fundamental transformation is attained due to its being divested of incidental impurities. The reality of this natural luminosity is obscured by adventitious impurities, yet what was not apparent at an earlier time will appear at a later point due to the power of the path.

COLOPHONS OF THE AUTHOR AND TRANSLATORS

This completes the *Stanzas of Distinguishing Phenomena from Their Intrinsic Nature* composed by the protector Maitreya.

This translation was prepared, edited, and established by the Kashmiri preceptor Mahājana and the lotsawa of Zhama, the monk Senge Gyaltsen.

COLOPHONS OF THE COMMENTATORS

These annotations were made by Shenphen Nangwa based on the commentary by the second buddha, Vasubandhu. Let there be excellent virtue!

Though not all were recorded as translated in the early translation period in indices of canonical texts such as the Denkarma, some accounts hold that all five Teachings of Maitreya were indeed translated at that time. Many great scholars lived in this period, including the abbot Śāntarakṣita and master Padmasambhava, and the Buddha's teachings still existed in their entirety in India. For these reasons they were undoubtedly translated in this period.

> With supreme intelligence, the regent and supreme bodhisattva
> Accurately explains the intent of the Victorious One's teachings.
> By the virtue of having explained this scripture, this gateway of
>   the Victorious One's heirs,
> May the immaculate teachings of the Victorious One spread in
>   the ten directions.
>
> The glacial lake of nonconceptual wakefulness
> Is the source of the treasures of the noble ones' Dharma.
> May I and all beings enter into it with delight
> And bring completion, maturation, and cultivation to
>   perfection.

In the Year of the Fire Ox I was requested to compose this text by Tulku Rinpoche at this very monastic center. At a later date I received the same request from some devoted individuals. Prompted by these requests and by my own devotion for this great treatise, I, Mipham Jamyang Nampar Gyelwa, later composed this commentary in the Year of the Wood Horse at the great monastic center of Katok, as a side project while explaining the *Ornament of Clear Realization*. I completed the text in three days. *Maṅgalam.*

APPENDIX
Ju Mipham's Topical Outline

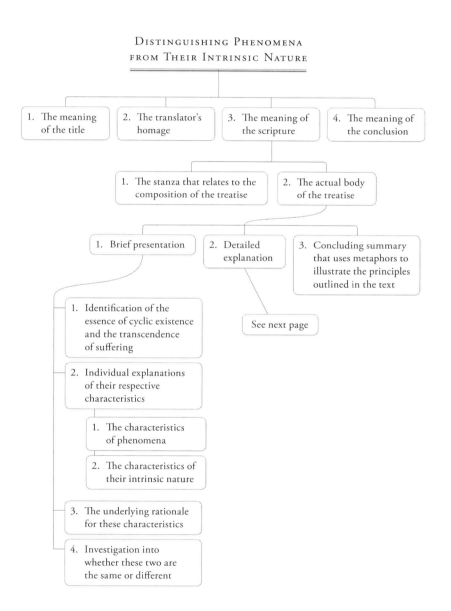

DISTINGUISHING PHENOMENA
FROM THEIR INTRINSIC NATURE

1. The meaning of the title

2. The translator's homage

3. The meaning of the scripture

4. The meaning of the conclusion

1. The stanza that relates to the composition of the treatise

2. The actual body of the treatise

1. Brief presentation

2. Detailed explanation

3. Concluding summary that uses metaphors to illustrate the principles outlined in the text

1. Identification of the essence of cyclic existence and the transcendence of suffering

2. Individual explanations of their respective characteristics

1. The characteristics of phenomena

2. The characteristics of their intrinsic nature

3. The underlying rationale for these characteristics

4. Investigation into whether these two are the same or different

See next page

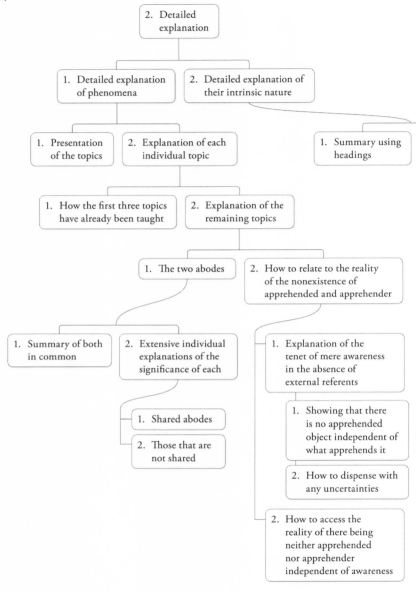

2. Detailed explanation of the meaning of these headings

1. The characteristics

2. The basis

3. Ascertainment

4. Contact

5. Recollection

6. Identification

1. Identification of the essence of the final, fundamental transformation

2. Detailed explanation of its unique features

1. Summary

2. Detailed explanation

1. Nature or essence

2. Entity or substance

3. Individuals

4. Distinct features

5. Requirements

6. Basis or support

7. Directing the mind

8. Application

9. Flaws

10. Benefits

See next page

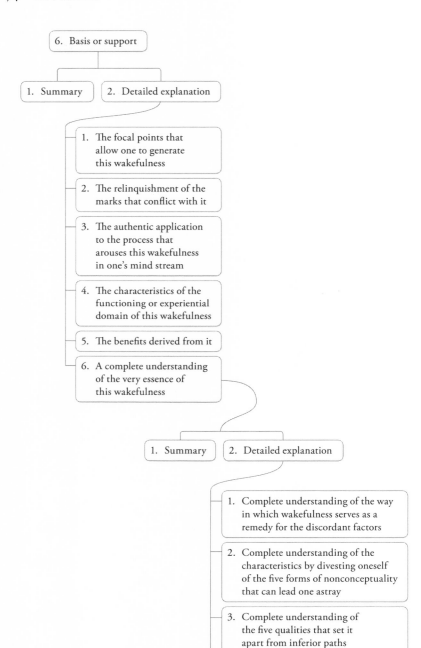

NOTES

INTRODUCTION

1. According to the Tibetan tradition these five are: *Ornament of Manifest Realization* (*Abhisa-mayālaṃkāra*), *Ornament of the Great Vehicle Sūtras* (*Mahāyānasūtrālaṃkāra*), *Distinguish-ing the Middle from Extremes* (*Madhyāntavibhāga*), *Distinguishing Phenomena from Their Intrinsic Nature* (*Dharmadharmatāvibhaṅga*), and the *Treatise on the Supreme Continuity* (*Uttaratantraśāstra/Ratnagotravibhāga*). In China and Japan the set of five is identified somewhat differently. See Mathes 1996, 16. See also this work for a survey and discussion of differing accounts, both ancient and modern, of the authorship of the Maitreya treatises.
2. Skt. *Dharmadharmatāvibhaṅga*; Tib. *Chos dang chos nyid rnam par 'byed pa.*
3. Shenphen Chökyi Nangwa (gzhan phan chos kyi snang ba, 1871–1927).
4. Ju Mipham ('ju mi pham, 1846–1912).
5. For a survey and discussion of differing accounts, both ancient and modern, of the identity of the author of the Maitreya treatises, see Mathes 1996.
6. Scott 2004.
7. Mathes 1996.
8. *sDe dge* edition of the Tibetan *Tripiṭaka,* text no. 4023.
9. gZhan 'phen chos kyi snang ba 1999.
10. 'Ju Mi pham 1990.

COMMENTARIES

1. The word Maitreya means "love."

ENGLISH-TIBETAN GLOSSARY

absence of marks	mtshan ma med pa
absence of self	bdag med
absorption	ting nge 'dzin
access	'jug pa
accomplishment	'grub pa
accumulation	tshogs
adventitious	lo bur ba
affliction	nyon mongs pa
afflictive obscuration	nyon sgrib
aggregate	phung po
all-ground	kun gzhi
appearance	snang ba
apprehend	'dzin pa, gzung ba
apprehended	gzung ba
apprehender	'dzin pa
aspect	cha, yan lag
aspiration	smon lam
attachment	chags pa
authentic	yang dag pa
awareness	rnam rig

basic field of phenomena	chos kyi dbyings
basis	gnas, gzhi
belief	lta ba
bodhisattva	byang chub sems dpa'
body of perfect enjoyment	long spyod rdzogs pa'i sku
body of qualities	chos kyi sku
Buddha, buddha	sangs rgyas

categorization	rnam grangs
cessation	'gog pa
characteristic	mtshan nyid
coarse	rags pa
cognitive obscuration	shes sgrib
collection of consciousness	rnam par shes pa'i tshogs
concentration	bsam gtan
concept	rtog pa, rnam rtog
conditioned	'dus byed
consciousness	rnam par shes pa
contact	reg pa
convention	tha snyad
craving	sred pa
cultivation	sgom pa
cyclic existence	'khor ba

dedication	sngo ba
defiling	zags bcas
denigration	skur 'debs
depreciation	skur 'debs
determination	yongs su gcod pa
devotion	mos pa
Dharma, dharma	chos
directing the mind	yid la byed pa
distinct	khyad par du 'phags pa, tha dad
distinction	khyad par
distraction	g.yeng ba
division	dbye ba
doubt	the tshom

effect	'bras bu
eliminate	spong ba
emanation body	sprul pa'i sku
emptiness	stong pa nyid
encounter	nye bar spyod pa
engage	'jug pa
enlightenment	byang chub
enlightenment, aspect of	byang chub kyi yan lag
entity	dngos po
equality	mnyam pa nyid
equilibrium	snyoms 'jug
equipoise	mnyam gzhag

error	phyin ci log pa
essence	ngo bo
essential nature	ngo bo nyid
establishment	grub pa
exaggerate	sgro btags pa
existence	yod pa, srid pa
experience	nye bar spyod pa, snang ba, myong ba
external object	phyi don
extreme	mtha'

factor of enlightenment	byang chub kyi phyogs
field	spyod yul, zhing
flaw	nyes pa
focus	dmigs pa
form	gzugs
formation	'du byed
foundation	gzhi
fruition	'bras bu
fundamental transformation	gnas yongs su gyur ba

genuine	yang dag pa
grasping	len pa
Great Vehicle	theg pa chen po
ground	gzhi, sa
ground of inspired conduct	mos spyod kyi sa

habitual tendency	bag chags
heat	dro ba

identity	bdag nyid
ignorance	ma rig pa
imaginary	kun brtags
imagination	kun rtog
insight	shes rab
intention	'dun pa
interest	mos pa
intrinsic nature	chos nyid

karma	las

Lesser Vehicle	theg pa dman pa
liberation	thar pa

listener	nyan thos
livelihood	'tsho ba
luminous	'od gsal ba

manifest	mngon gyur
mark	mtshan ma
mastery	dbang ba
meaning	don
means	thabs
meditation	sgom pa
meditative absorption	ting nge 'dzin
meditative equipoise	mnyam gzhag
mental state	sems byung
method	thabs
mind	blo, sems
mind stream	rgyud
mistaken	phyin ci log pa
mundane	'jig rten pa

nature	don, rang bzhin
noble	'phags pa
nonconceptual wakefulness	rnam par mi rtog pa'i ye shes
nonconceptuality	rnam par mi rtog pa
nonexistence	med pa

object	don, yul
obscuration	sgrib pa
observation	dmigs pa

particularity	khyad par
path	lam
path of accumulation	tshogs lam
path of cultivation	sgom lam
path of joining	sbyor lam
path of no more training	mi slob lam
path of seeing	mthong lam
perception, direct	mngon sum
perpetuation	nyer len pa
phenomenon	chos
power	stobs
practices	grub pa, 'jug pa
principle	rnam grangs, rnam gzhag

property	chos
purification, complete	rnam byang
purity	rnam par dag pa

quality	chos, yon tan

rationale	'thad pa
real	bden pa, yang dag pa
reality	de kho na nyid, don
realization	rtogs pa
realm	khams, gnas
reasonable	'thad pa
relative	kun rdzob
relinquish	spong ba
remedy	gnyen po
result	'bras bu

self-realized buddha	rang sangs rgyas
sentient being	sems can
significance	don
stain	dri ma
stream of being	rgyud
study	thos pa
subject	chos can, yul can
subsequent attainment	rjes thob
substance	rdzas
subtle	phra ba
suchness	de bzhin nyid
superimposition	sgro btags
superior	khyad par du 'phags pa
superknowledge	mngon shes
supramundane	'jig rten las 'das pa

tenet	grub mtha'
thoroughly established [nature]	yongs grub
thought	rtog pa, rnam rtog
trainings	gom pa, slob pa
transcendence	'das pa, pha rol du phyin pa
true	bden pa, yang dag pa

ultimate	don dam
unconditioned	'dus ma byed
unmistaken	phyin ci ma log pa

view	lta ba
virtue	dge ba

wakefulness	ye shes
world	'jig rten
world of the environment	gnod kyi 'jig rten

TIBETAN-ENGLISH-SANSKRIT GLOSSARY

kun btags	imputed	parikalpita
kun rtog	imagination	parikalpa
kun brtags	imaginary, imputed	parikalpita
kun rdzob	relative	saṃvṛti
kun gzhi	all-ground	ālaya
skur 'debs	denigration, depreciation	apavāda
skye mched	sense source	āyatana
khams	element, realm	dhātu
khyad par	distinction, particularity	viśeṣa
khyad par du 'phags pa	distinct, superior	viśiṣṭa, vaiśeṣika
mkhas pa	expert	kauśalya
'khor ba	cyclic existence	saṃsāra
grub mtha'	tenet	siddhānta
dge ba	virtue	kuśala, śubha
'gog pa	cessation	nirodha

Tibetan	English	Sanskrit
'grub pa	accomplishment, establishment	niṣpatti, prasiddha, siddhi
rgod pa	agitation	uddhata, auddhatya
rgyud	[mind] stream, stream of being	santāna
sgom pa	cultivation, meditation, training	bhāvanā
sgrib pa	obscuration	āvaraṇa, āvṛti, chādana, nivaraṇa
sgrub pa	practice	pratipatti, prapatti, prapan natā, sādhana
sgro btags	exaggeration, superimposition	āropa, samāropa
sgom spang	eliminated through cultivation	bhāvanāheya
sgom lam	path of cultivation	bhāvanāmārga
nga rgyal	pride	abhimāna, unnati, māna
ngo bo	essence	svabhāva
ngo bo nyid	essential nature	svabhāva, svābhāvikatva
dngos po	entity	bhāva, vastu
mngon gyur	manifest	abhimukhi
mngon shes	superknowledge	abhijñā
mngon sum	perception, direct	pratyakṣa
sngo ba	dedication	nati
chags pa	attachment	sakti
chos	dharma, phenomenon, property, quality	dharma
chos kyi sku	body of qualities	dharmakāya
chos kyi dbyings	basic space of phenomena	dharmadhātu
chos can	subject	dharmin
chos mchog	supreme property	agradharma
chos nyid	intrinsic nature	dharmatā

'jig rten	world	loka
'jig rten pa	of the world, mundane	laukika
'jig rten las 'das pa	beyond the world, supramundane	lokottara
'jug pa	access, engage, practice	avakrānti, avatṛ, praviś-, praveśa, pravṛt-, visāra, sār
rjes thob	subsequent attainment	pṛṣṭhalabdha
rjes dpag	inference	anumāna
nyan thos	listener	śrāvaka
nye bar spyod pa	experience, encounter	upabhoga
nyer len	appropriation, perpetuation	upādāna
nyes pa	flaw	doṣa
nyon sgrib	afflictive obscuration	kleśāvaraṇa
nyon mongs pa	affliction	kleśa
gnyen po	remedy	pratipakṣa, vipakṣa
mnyam pa nyid	equality	samatā
mnyam gzhag	[meditative] equipoise	samādhā
snyoms 'jug	equilibrium	samāpatti
ting nge 'dzin	absorption, meditative absorption	samādhi
rten 'brel	dependent origination	pratītyasamutpāda
rtog pa	concept, thought	kalpanā
rtogs pa	realization	adhigama, anubudhyana, anubodha, praveśa
lta ba	belief, view	darśana, dṛṣṭi
stong pa nyid	emptiness	śūnyatā
stobs	power	bala
tha snyad	convention	vyavahāra
thabs	means, method	upāya

thar pa	liberation	mokṣa
the tshom	doubt	vicikitsā
theg pa chen po	Great Vehicle	mahāyāna
theg pa dman pa	Lesser Vehicle	hīnayāna
thos pa	study	śruta
mtha'	extreme	anta
mthun phyogs	conducive factor	sapakṣa
mthong lam	path of seeing	darśanamārga
'thad pa	reasonable	upapatti

dag pa	purity	śuddhi
dad pa	faith	śraddhā
de kho na nyid	reality	tattva
de bzhin nyid	suchness	tathatā
don	object, meaning, nature, reality, significance	artha, bhāva
don dam	ultimate	paramārtha
dran pa	mindfulness	mṛti
dran pa nye bar bzhag pa	application of mindfulness	smṛty-upasthāna
dri ma	stain	mala
dri med	stainless	amala, nirmala
dro ba	heat	uṣma
bdag	self	ātman
bdag nyid	identity	ātman
bdag med	absence of self	nairātmya
bden pa	real, true	sat
'du byed	formation	saṃskāra
'dun pa	intention	chanda

		saṃskṛta
'dus byed	conditioned	saṃskṛta
'dus ma byed	unconditioned	asaṃskṛta
gnas	basis, realm, state	adhiṣṭhāna, avasthā, āśraya, pratiṣṭhā, sanniśraya, sthāna, sthiti
gnas ngan len	negative tendency	dauṣṭhulya
gnas yongs su gyur ba	fundamental transformation	āśrayaparāvṛtti
rnam grangs	categorization, principle	paryāya
rnam rtog	concept, thought	vikalpa
rnam par dag pa	purity	viśuddhi
rnam par mi rtog pa	nonconceptuality	avikalpana, nirvikalpa
rnam par mi rtog pa'i ye shes	nonconceptual wakefulness	avikalpana jñāna, nirvikalpa jñāna
rnam par shes pa	consciousness	vijñāna
rnam par shes pa'i tshogs	collection of consciousness	vijñānakāya
rnam byang	purification, complete	vyavadāna
rnam smin	ripening	vipāka
rnam gzhag	classification, principle	vyavasthāna, vyavasthāpana
rnam rig	awareness	vijñapti
rnal 'byor	spiritual practice	yoga
snang ba	appearance, experience	darśana, prakhyāna, pratibhās-, pratibhāsa
gnod	vessel	bhājana
gnod kyi 'jig rten	world of the environment	bhājanaloka
spang bya	eliminated factor	prahātavya, heya
spong ba	elimination, relinquishment	tyāga, prahāṇa, vivarjana
spyod yul	field	gocara
sprul pa'i sku	emanation body	nirmāṇakāya
spros bral	freedom from conceptual constructs	niṣprapañca

pha rol du phyin pa	transcendence	pāramitā
phung po	aggregate	skandha
phyi don	external object	bāhyārtha
phyin ci ma log pa	unmistaken	aviparīta, aviparyasta
phyin ci log pa	error, mistaken	viparyasta, viparyāsa
phra ba	subtle	sūkṣma
'phags pa	noble	ārya
'phags lam yan lag	aspect of the noble path	āryamārgāṅga
bag chags	habitual tendency	vāsanā
byang chub	enlightenment	bodhi
byang chub kyi phyogs	factor of enlightenment	bodhipakṣya
byang chub kyi yan lag	aspect of enlightenment	bodhyaṅga
byang chub sems dpa'	bodhisattva	bodhisattva
bying ba	dullness	laya
dbang po	faculty	indriya
dbang ba	mastery	vaśitā
dbye ba	division	bheda
sbyin pa	generosity	dāna
sbyor lam	path of joining	prayogamārga
'bras bu	fruition, result, effect	phala
ma rig pa	ignorance	avidyā
mi mthun phyogs	discordant factor	vipakṣa
mi slob lam	path of no more training	aśaikṣamārga
med pa	absence, nonexistence	abhāva, asat, asattva
mos pa	devotion, inspiration, interest	adhimukti, adhimokṣa

mos spyod kyi sa	ground of inspired conduct	adhimukticaryābhūmi
dmigs pa	focus, observation	ālambana, upalabdhi, upalambha
smon lam	aspiration	praṇidhāna
rtse mo	summit	mūrdhāna
brtson 'grus	diligence	vīrya
tshul khrims	discipline	śīla
tshogs	accumulation	kāya, sambhāra
tshogs lam	path of accumulation	sambhāramārga
mtshan nyid	characteristic	lakṣaṇa
mtshan ma	mark	nimitta
mtshan ma med pa	absence of marks	ānimittā, nimittābhāva, nirnimittatā
'tsho ba	livelihood	ājīva
'dzin pa	apprehend, apprehender	grahaṇa, grāha, grāhaka
rdzas	substance	dravya, upadhi
zhi gnas	calm abiding	śamatha
gzhan dbang	dependent [nature]	paratantra
gzhi	basis, ground, foundation	ādhāra, nidhāna, vastu
zags bcas	defiling	sāsrava
gzugs	form	rūpa
gzung ba	apprehend, apprehended	grāhya
bzod pa	acceptance, patience	kṣānti
'od gsal ba	luminous	prabhāsvara

Tibetan	English	Sanskrit
yang dag pa	authentic, genuine, real, true	bhūta
yan lag	aspect	aṅga
yid la byed pa	directing the mind	manaskāraṇa, manasikāra, manasikriyā, manaskāra
yul	object	viṣaya
yul can	subject	viṣayin
ye shes	wakefulness	jñāna
yongs grub	thoroughly established [nature]	pariniṣpatti, pariniṣpanna
yongs su gcod pa	determination	pariccheda
yod pa	existence	astitva, bhāva, sadbhāva
yon tan	good quality, quality .	guṇa
gyeng ba	distraction	vikṣepa
rags pa	coarse	udāra, audārika
rang bzhin	nature	prakṛti, svabhāva
rang sangs rgyas	self-realized buddha	pratyekabuddha
reg pa	contact	sparśa
lam	path	pratipad, pratipatti, mārga
las	karma	karman
las kyi mtha'	activity	karmānta
len pa	grasping	upādāna
lo bur ba	adventitious	āgantuka
log lta	mistaken view	mithyādṛṣṭi
long spyod rdzogs pa'i sku	body of perfect enjoyment	saṃbhogakāya, sāmbhogikakāya
shin tu sbyangs ba	agility	praśrabdhi
shes sgrib	cognitive obscuration	jñeyāvaraṇa
shes bzhin	alertness	saṃprajanya

shes rab	insight	prajñā
sa	ground	bhūmi
sangs rgyas	buddha	buddha
sems	mind	citta, cetas
sems bskyed	development of the enlightened mind	cittotpāda
sems can	sentient being	sattva
sems byung	mental state	caitta
srid pa	existence, becoming	bhava, sambhava
sred pa	craving	tṛṣṇā
slob pa	training	śaikṣa
bsam gtan	concentration	dhyāna

BIBLIOGRAPHY

SŪTRAS

Prophecy Requested by Kāśyapa (*Kāśyapaparivarta*). D* 87.
Sūtra of the Journey to Laṅkā (*Laṅkāvatāra*). D 107.
Sūtra Requested by Maitreya (Tib. *mDo byams zhus*). Chapter 72 in the *Transcendent Insight in Twenty-five Thousand Lines* (*Pañcaviṁśatikasāhasrikā-prajñāpāramitā*), D 10; or chapter 83 in the *Transcendent Insight in Eighteen Thousand Lines* (*Aṣṭādaśasāhasrikā-prajñāpāramitā*), D 9.
Sūtra That Teaches the Dhāraṇī of Nonconceptuality (*Avikalpapraveśa-nāma-dhāraṇī*). D 142.

CLASSICAL INDIAN AND TIBETAN TEXTS

Maitreya. *dBus dang mtha' rnam par 'byed pa* (*Madhyāntavibhāga*). D 4021.
_____. *Chos dang chos nyid rnam par 'byed pa* (*Dharmadharmatāvibhaṅga*). D 4023.
_____. *rGyud bla ma* (*Mahāyānottaratantra-śāstra, Ratnagotravibhāga*). D 4024.
_____. *mNgon par rtogs pa'i rgyan* (*Abhisamayālaṁkāra*). D 3786.
_____. *Theg pa chen po'i mdo sde'i rgyan* (*Mahāyānasūtrālaṁkāra*). D 4020.
'Ju Mi pham. 1990. *Chos dang chos nyid rnam par 'byed pa'i tshig leur byas pa'i 'grel pa ye shes snang ba rnam 'byed*. In *Sde-dge dgon-chen Prints of the Writings of 'Jam-mgon 'Ju Mi-pham-rgya-mtsho*, ed. Dilgo Khyentse, vol. 4, 609-57. Kathmandu: Shechen Monastery, 1990.
Vasubandhu. *Chos dang chos nyid rnam par 'byed pa'i 'grel pa*. D 4028.
gZhan 'phen chos kyi snang ba. 1999. *Chos dang chos nyid rnam par 'byed pa'i mchan 'grel*, ed. Tarthang Tulku Rinpoche. Berkeley: Yeshe De Project, 1999.

---

* Enumeration according to the *sDe dge* edition of the Tibetan canon.

RECENT STUDIES AND TRANSLATIONS

Brunnhölzl, Karl. 2012. *Mining for Wisdom within Delusion: Maitreya's* Distinction between Phenomena and the Nature of Phenomena *and Its Indian and Tibetan Commentaries.* Boston: Snow Lion.

Dharmachakra Translation Committee, trans. 2006. *Middle Beyond Extremes: Maitreya's* Madhyāntavibhāga *with commentaries by Khenpo Shenga and Ju Mipham.* Ithaca: Snow Lion Publications.

Duckworth, Douglas. 2008. *Mipam on Buddha-Nature: The Ground of the Nyingma Tradition.* Albany: SUNY Press.

_____. 2011. *Jamgön Mipam: His Life and Teachings.* Boston: Shambhala.

Mathes, Klaus-Dieter. 1996. *Unterscheidung der Gegebenheiten von ihrem wahren Wesen (Dharmadharmatāvibhāga).* Indica et Tibetica 26. Swisttal-Odendorf: Indica et Tibetica Verlag.

Scott, Jim, trans. 2004. *Maitreya's* Distinguishing Phenomena and Pure Being *with Commentary by Mipham.* Ithaca: Snow Lion Publications.

Robertson, Raymond E. 2007–. *A Study of the* Dharmadharmatāvibhaṅga. 4 vols. Beijing: China Tibetology Publishing House.

INDEX